Consorts of the Caliphs

Letter from the General Editor

The Library of Arabic Literature series offers Arabic editions and English translations of significant works of Arabic literature, with an emphasis on the seventh to nineteenth centuries. The Library of Arabic Literature thus includes texts from the pre-Islamic era to the cusp of the modern period, and encompasses a wide range of genres, including poetry, poetics, fiction, religion, philosophy, law, science, history, and historiography.

Books in the series are edited and translated by internationally recognized scholars and are published in parallel-text format with Arabic and English on facing pages, and are also made available as English-only paperbacks.

The Library encourages scholars to produce authoritative, though not necessarily critical, Arabic editions, accompanied by modern, lucid English translations. Its ultimate goal is to introduce the rich, largely untapped Arabic literary heritage to both a general audience of readers as well as to scholars and students.

The Library of Arabic Literature is supported by a grant from the New York University Abu Dhabi Institute and is published by NYU Press.

Philip F. Kennedy
General Editor, Library of Arabic Literature

About this Paperback

This paperback edition differs in a few respects from its dual-language hardcover predecessor. Because of the compact trim size the pagination has changed, but paragraph numbering has been retained to facilitate cross-referencing with the hardcover. Material that referred to the Arabic edition has been updated to reflect the English-only format, and other material has been corrected and updated where appropriate. For information about the Arabic edition on which this English translation is based and about how the LAL Arabic text was established, readers are referred to the hardcover.

Consorts of the Caliphs

Women and the Court of Baghdad

BY

Ibn al-Sāʿī

TRANSLATED BY

Shawkat M. Toorawa and the Editors of the Library of Arabic Literature

INTRODUCTION BY

Julia Bray

FOREWORD BY

Marina Warner

VOLUME EDITOR

Julia Bray

NEW YORK UNIVERSITY PRESS
New York

NEW YORK UNIVERSITY PRESS
New York

The Library of Congress has catalogued the hardback edition as follows:

Ibn al-Saʿi, ʿAli ibn Anjab, 1196 or 1197–1275.
Consorts of the caliphs : women and the court of Baghdad / Ibn al-Saʿi ; edited by Shawkat M. Toorawa ; translated by the editors of the Library of Arabic Literature ; introduction by Julia Bray ; foreword by Marina Warner ; volume editor Julia Bray.
pages cm. — (Library of Arabic Literature)
Bilingual English and Arabic texts on facing pages.
Includes bibliographical references and indexes.
ISBN 978-1-4798-5098-3 (cl : alk. paper) — ISBN 978-1-4798-4236-0 (e-book) — ISBN 978-1-4798-7904-5 (e-book)
1. Women—Islamic Empire—Anecdotes—Early works to 1800. 2. Queens—Islamic Empire—Anecdotes—Early works to 1800. 3. Islamic Empire—History—750–1258 Early works to 1800. 4. Abbasids—Early works to 1800.
I. Toorawa, Shawkat M., editor. II. Bray, Julia, editor. III. Ibn al-Saʿi, ʿAli ibn Anjab, 1196 or 1197–1275. Nisaʾ al-khulafaʾ. IV. Ibn al-Saʿi, ʿAli ibn Anjab, 1196 or 1197–1275. Nisaʾ al-khulafaʾ. English. V. Title.
DS38.4.A2I25413 2015
909'.097670109252—dc23 2014044217

ISBN 978-1-4798-6679-3 (pb : alk. paper)
ISBN 978-1-4798-3657-4 (e-book)
ISBN 978-1-4798-0477-1 (e-book)

New York University Press books are printed on acid-free paper, and their binding materials are chosen for strength and durability.

Series design and composition by Nicole Hayward
Typeset in Adobe Text

Manufactured in the United States of America

10 9 8 7 6 5 4 3 2 1

Contents

Abbreviations

AD	*anno Domini* = Gregorian (Christian) year
AH	*anno Hegirae* = Hijrah (Muslim) year
art.	article
Ar.	Arabic
c.	century
ca.	circa = about, approximately
cf.	confer = compare
d.	died
ed.	editor, edition, edited by
EI2	*Encyclopaedia of Islam*, Second edition
EI3	*Encyclopaedia of Islam, Three* [Third edition]
EIran	*Encyclopaedia Iranica*
esp.	especially
f., ff.	folio, folios
fl.	flourished
lit.	literally
MS	manuscript
n.	note
n.d.	no date
n.p.	no place
no.	number
p., pp.	page, pages
pl.	plural
Q	Qur'an
r.	ruled
vol., vols.	volume, volumes

Foreword

MARINA WARNER

"Muted" was the epithet used to describe female subjects by the anthropologists Edwin and Shirley Ardener in an influential critique of their discipline and its methods, published in 1975; they identified a systemic problem, that fieldworkers consistently sought out the men's story, set down what they heard, and attended above all to male activities; in most cases, the researchers had little access to women, but they also did not try to listen to them or elicit their stories.[1] Consequently, women disappeared from the record, their voices were not registered, and the whole picture suffered from distortion.

The Ardeners provided a polemical but persuasive angle of view on a widespread discomfort with cultural assumptions, and their work spurred a new generation of readers and researchers to begin listening in to "muted groups" of individuals from the past, those muffled female participants whose "labour created our world" (to borrow Angela Carter's phrase about storytellers, ballad-singers, and other cultural keepers of memory). The impulse was part of the broadly feminist program of those years, but it grew larger than that political movement, as scholars in history, literature, social studies, and indeed almost every area of inquiry pursued the new archaeology, unearthing remarkable new material about women's lives and deeds, and often bringing forgotten figures back to consciousness. The findings did not only fill in gaps in the view, but also transformed the whole horizon and realigned contemporary understanding in crucial ways. Historians such as Natalie Zemon Davis and Emmanuel Le Roy Ladurie excavated provincial archives and tuned in to the voices of female witnesses and defendants; literary scholars returned to and in some cases revived familiar and not unsuccessful writers (Christine de Pisan, Christina Rossetti, Emily Dickinson) to illuminate the social and psychological radiation of their works as women. Some of the ignorance—and the bigotry that arises from ignorance—began to lift, with many powerful reverberations for the position of women today. It is sobering to remember that less than a hundred years ago, Oxford and Cambridge did not award degrees to women (until 1920 and 1947 respectively), though they had begun to allow women to sit (successfully) for the exams. Now women have reached numerical parity at undergraduate and graduate levels in many subjects, and have entered every discipline as teachers and professors—Maryam Mirzakhani has won the Fields Medal in Mathematics and Julia Bray holds the Laudian Chair of Arabic at Oxford. (I do realize that Julia Bray, as project editor of this volume, may dislike being singled out for praise, but her appointment seems to me a great cause for pride and pleasure, and so I hope she will not mind my drawing attention to it.)

If low expectations, combined with misunderstanding and social prejudice, have muted women in the Western tradition, the silence that has wrapped women in the East is even deeper. In the United States and Europe, the voices of women from the Islamic past are often eroticized and trivialized—through harem romances and desert epics, advertising and propaganda. Rimsky-Korsakov's luscious music for *Shéhérazade* was adapted for Fokine's ballet of 1910 and accompanies a plot in which orientalist assumptions of savagery, lasciviousness, slavery, and tyranny are taken to torrid extremes. Ways of selecting and presenting stories from the *Arabian Nights* have exacerbated the problem: heroines who are adventurous and courageous and have strong, interior passions and resourceful ideas (Zumurrud, Badr, Tawaddud, and many others—they abound in the work) were overlooked in favor of the insipid love interest, like the princess in *Aladdin*, who is almost entirely silent and, when she does speak, foolish. Collections of the *Arabian Nights* selected for children frequently cut the frame tale and present the Nights as a bunch of stories, without the decisive organizing principle provided by Shahrazad's stratagem, thus muting the female storyteller as pictured in the book and omitting the crucial rationale, her ransom tale-telling.

Consorts of the Caliphs is a work of historical biography, not an anthology of fictions, and it gives voice to the spirited, learned, influential women of the medieval past in the Abbasid empire. It unbinds our ears and eyes to some of what they said and did. The author/compiler Ibn al-Sāʿī was himself a poet and a librarian, and through patient sifting of archival memories, both oral and written, he communicates precious echoes and fragments from a period spanning five hundred years: the earliest woman whose life he sets before us was the wife of Caliph al-Manṣūr (reigned 136–58/754–75), while the latest, Shāhān, died in 652/1254–55. In the entry on Zubaydah, who died in 532/1137–38, Ibn al-Sāʿī's epitaph is brief: "She was lovely and praised for her beauty." This is uncharacteristically reticent. For the early years, Ibn al-Sāʿī fills in the blanks with stories he has gathered from chains of sources; for the later period, within living memory, he passes on what he has heard. Women's words rise from the page in many registers—passionate high poetry, mordant quips and sallies, and prayerful thoughts. The effect is vivid and fleeting, a series of lantern slides within a laconic yet impassioned account that comes across clearly now and again but then breaks up or fades. Slaves, "dependents," lovers and wives are glimpsed—dazzlingly accomplished individuals in some cases, who survive by their wits, risking all with their tongues; their adopted sobriquets give a flavor of their spiritedness: Ghādir ("Inconstance"), Ghaḍīḍ ("Luscious"), Qurrat al-ʿAyn ("Solace"), Ḍirār ("Damage"), Sarīrah ("Secret"), and even Qabīḥah ("Ugly").

In other cases, the women, august or beggared, full of years or plucked before their time, pass by in a roll of honor, on a pervasive note of reverence and elegy. Ibn al-Sāʿī's book conveys their mobility, the complexity of the roles they fulfilled, the variety of their ethnic and religious origins, and their high status. Their circumstances reveal the intermingling of ethnic origins and faiths. The term "slave" itself, used here after careful thought on the part of the translators and their editors, clearly needs more attention from historians, since the term, as habitually used in English, does not capture the ambiguities in the situation of Faḍl, for example, whose raunchy flytings the translators have met with matching boldness:[2]

He moaned and groaned and whined all night,
And creaked just like a door-hinge.

Some of Ibn al-Sāʿī's material reads like fabulist literature. Anecdotes and personalities have intermingled with the stories of the *Arabian Nights* and grown into the stuff of legend: the passion of Maḥbūbah and al-Mutawakkil, for instance, a brief, dramatic tale of mutual dreaming and reconciliation, appears in the complete cycle of the *Arabian Nights* (as rendered by Malcolm Lyons for Penguin or Jamel Eddine Bencheikh and André Miquel for the Pléiade). Hārūn al-Rashīd and the Barmakids, including the vizier Jaʿfar, have become mythic as well as historical heroes. However, the historically-minded author of *Consorts of the Caliphs* is also an accountant, and the enormous prices paid (one hundred thousand gold dinars to the slave ʿArīb for her own slave Bidʿah, for example) or spent on wedding gifts (thousands of pearls and heavy candles of ambergris for Būrān) are entered admiringly into the record. Munificence of this princely order occurs in the *Arabian Nights*, but it is rarely bestowed by powerful women, as we see here: even women who are slaves, if in favor, can dispose of treasure as they wish. This contradiction is one of myriad social details that raise further questions about the nature of women's subjugation in the oriental, and specifically Abbasid, past.

This volume is the sixteenth title in the Library of Arabic Literature, and a most valuable addition to an invaluable series that is revolutionizing access to the corpus for non-Arabic readers like myself as well as establishing meticulous editions for those who can read the works in the original language. Ibn al-Sāʿī's gallery of women poets, wits, singers, chess players, teachers, benefactors, and builders (of waterways, libraries, and law schools) transcends the collective, stereotypical character of great ladies as femmes fatales, wives, mothers, or concubines; his report lifts a veil of silence and allows us to overhear the hum of lyric, argument, wit, and elegy from women's voices in the past. Its rich retrievals will prove marvelously inspiring, both for scholarship and for other creative work. One might dream of a new opera—about ʿInān? about Faḍl? about Būrān?—to do justice to the women who sing out from Ibn al-Sāʿī's revelatory and enjoyable archive.

Marina Warner

Acknowledgments

SHAWKAT M. TOORAWA

We are grateful to the members of the collaborative academic alliance Radical Reassessment of Arabic Arts, Language, and Literature (RRAALL) for passing the *Consorts of the Caliphs* translation project on to the Library of Arabic Literature (LAL), and in particular to Joseph Lowry, the project's *spiritus auctor*, who has been tirelessly committed to it.

We would like to thank Ian Stevens for early encouragement; Muhammet Günaydın of Istanbul University for obtaining a copy of the manuscript; and Gila Waels, along with Nora Yousif, Manal Demaghlatrous, Antoine El Khayat, and Farhana Goha, for cheerful and expert assistance in Abu Dhabi. The feedback we received from audience members at the public panel discussion "Caliphs and their Consorts: Translating Anecdotes and Poetry in Ibn al-Sāʿī's *Nisāʾ al-Khulafāʾ*" in December 2012 in Abu Dhabi was immensely helpful—especially as we were reminded how important it is to translate for *readers*, not just for ourselves. The expert feedback of Richard Sieburth was invaluable, as were the participation of Maurice Pomerantz and Justin Stearns in an intensive translation workshop in Abu Dhabi in December 2013. Everyone at NYU Abu Dhabi and at NYU Press has been unfailingly supportive of us and of LAL.

•

I am grateful to RRAALL for nurturing in me a love of collaboration in scholarship and to Philip Kennedy for turning the fantasy of the Library of Arabic Literature into reality and including me in that fantasy/reality. I know I must have done something right for so much of my "work" now to involve spending time in the superlative company of Philip Kennedy and James Montgomery. When you add Devin Stewart, Tahera Qutbuddin, Joseph Lowry, Michael Cooperson, and Julia Bray to the mix, the company becomes unmatchable.

I must single out Julia. Not only did she save me from all manner of goofs and gaffes as I prepared the Arabic edition, and not only did her meticulous attention to every single word in this volume make it vastly superior—she also provided me with the opportunity to collaborate, on a daily basis, with a consummate scholar and a dear friend. For this I am truly grateful.

It has also been an honor to work with the outstanding scholar-translator-manager-editor-gentleman Chip Rossetti, the wonderful and resourceful LAL aide and assistant editor Gemma Juan-Simó, and our magician of a digital production manager, Stuart Brown. Martin Grosch's and Jennifer Ilius's maps adorn the volume beautifully, and Rana Siblini, Wiam El-Tamami, Marie Deer, and Elias Saba contributed invisibly but crucially. And Nicole Hayward's design of the LAL paperbacks is simply gorgeous.

My new homes, the Department of Near Eastern Languages & Civilizations and Yale University, have been welcoming and supportive.

As for my family—Parvine, Maryam, Asiya (and Cotomili)—they are spectacular in indulging my obsessions and provide a constant and welcome reminder of what is truly important.

Shawkat M. Toorawa

Introduction

JULIA BRAY

Tāj al-Dīn ʿAlī ibn Anjab Ibn al-Sāʿī (593–674/1197–1276) was a Baghdadi man of letters and historian. As the librarian of two great law colleges, the Niẓāmiyyah and later the Munstanṣiriyyah, and a protégé of highly placed members of the regime, Ibn al-Sāʿī enjoyed privileged access to the ruling circles and official archives of the caliphate[4] and contributed to the great cultural resurgence that took place under the last rulers of the Abbasid dynasty. This was an age of historians, and most of Ibn al-Sāʿī's works were histories of one sort or another, but only fragments survive. The only one of his works that has come down to us complete is *Consorts of the Caliphs*. This too is a history insofar as it follows a rough chronological order, but in other respects it is more like a sub-genre of the biographical dictionary. It consists of brief life sketches, with no narrative interconnection, of concubines and wives of the Abbasid caliphs and, in an appendix, consorts of "viziers and military commanders." This last section, however, is slightly muddled; it includes some concubines of caliphs and wives of two Saljūq sultans, as well as one woman who was neither;[5] has a duplicate entry; and is not chronological, all of which suggests that it is a draft.[6]

For the later Abbasid ladies of *Consorts of the Caliphs*, Ibn al-Sāʿī uses his own sources and insider knowledge, but for the earlier ones, he quotes well-known literary materials, drawing especially on the supreme historian of early Abbasid court literature, Abū l-Faraj al-Iṣfahānī (284–ca. 363/897–ca. 972), author of the *Book of Songs*

(*Kitāb al-Aghānī*). In this way, two quite different formats are juxtaposed in *Consorts of the Caliphs*: the later entries follow the obituary format of the chronicles of Ibn al-Sāʿī's period; the earlier ones are adapted from the classical anecdote format of several centuries before, which combined narrative and verse in dramatic scenes. Many of the entries from both periods are framed by *isnād*s—the names of the people who originally recorded the anecdotes and of the people who then transmitted them, either by word of mouth or by reading from an authorized text. The names of Ibn al-Sāʿī's own informants give an indication of what interested scholars and litterateurs in the Baghdad of his day. The meticulousness of the *isnād*s signals that *Consorts of the Caliphs* is a work of serious scholarship, as does the fact that Ibn al-Sāʿī's personal informants are men of considerable standing.[7]

Ibn al-Sāʿī survived the Mongol sack of Baghdad in 656/1258 and lived on unmolested under Ilkhanid rule. *Consorts of the Caliphs*, which was written shortly before 1258,[8] survives in a single late-fifteenth-century manuscript.[9] This one small work is unique in affording multiple perspectives on things that have, over the centuries, been felt to be fundamental and durable in the Arabic literary and cultural imagination: the poetry of the heroines of early Abbasid culture; the mid-Abbasid casting of their careers and love lives into legend; a reimagining of the court life of the Abbasid period, along with the idealization of the court life of their own times, by Ibn al-Sāʿī and his contemporaries; and finally, the perspective of some two hundred years later in which the stories retold by Ibn al-Sāʿī were still valued, but lumped together in a single manuscript with an unrelated and unauthored miscellany of wit, wisdom, poems, and anecdotes.[10]

Ibn al-Sāʿī's Life and Times: Post- and Pre-Mongol

What is it like to live through a cataclysm? When Ibn al-Sāʿī finished writing his *Brief Lives of the Caliphs* (*Mukhtaṣar akhbār al-khulafāʾ*) in 666/1267–68 (as he notes on the last page),[11] it was as a survivor of the Mongol sack of Baghdad ten years earlier, in which the thirty-seventh and last ruling Abbasid caliph, al-Mustaʿṣim, had been killed. With al-Mustaʿṣim's death came the end of the caliphate, an institution that had lasted more than half a millennium. Although the caliphate had shrunk by the end from an empire to a rump, the Abbasid caliphs, as descendants of the Prophet's uncle, still claimed to be the lawful rulers of all Muslims. The late Abbasids ruled as well as reigned, asserting their claim to universal leadership by propounding an all-inclusive Sunnism and bonding with the growing groundswell of Sufism.[12] Baghdad remained the intellectual and cultural capital of Arabic speakers everywhere.

After the Mongols arrived, all this changed. Egypt's Mamluk rulers—Turkic slave soldiers—became the new Sunni standard-bearers, and Baghdad lost its role as the seat of high courtly culture. Ibn al-Sāʿī wrote *Brief Lives* in full consciousness of the new world order. The work dwells on the zenith of the caliphate centuries before and tells stirring tales of the great, early Abbasids, underlined by poetry. This is legendary history, cultural memory. After noting how the streets of Baghdad ran with blood after the death of al-Mustaʿṣim,[13] Ibn al-Sāʿī recites an elegiac tally of the genealogy, names, and regnal titles of the whole fateful Abbasid dynasty, of whom every sixth caliph was to be murdered or deposed.[14] The tailpiece of *Brief Lives*, by contrast, an enumeration of the world's remaining Muslim rulers, is a prosaic political geography.[15] Baghdad no longer rates a mention on the world stage. Culture is not evoked. The question that hangs unasked is: what was left to connect the past to the present?

Consorts of the Caliphs, Both Free and Slave, to give it its full title, is a kind of anticipated answer to that question. It is an essay in cultural memory written in the reign of al-Mustaʿṣim,[16] but it shows no premonition of danger, even though the Mongols were already on the march. It represents the last two hundred years—the reigns of al-Muqtadī (467–87/1075–94), al-Mustaẓhir (487–512/1094–1118), al-Mustaḍīʾ (566–75/1170–80), al-Nāṣir li-Dīn Allāh

(575–622/1180–1225), al-Ẓāhir (622–23/1225–26), al-Mustanṣir (623–40/1226–42), and the beginning of the reign of al-Mustaʿṣim (640–56/1242–58)—as a golden age for the lucky citizens of Baghdad, thanks to the public benefactions of the great ladies of the caliph's household.[17] It is a miniature collection of vignettes juxtaposed with no reference to the general fabric of events, designed as a twin to Ibn al-Sāʿī's now lost *Lives of Those Gracious and Bounteous Consorts of Caliphs Who Lived to See Their Own Sons Become Caliph* (*Kitāb Akhbār man adrakat khilāfat waladihā min jihāt al-khulafāʾ dhawāt al-maʿrūf wa-l-ʿaṭāʾ*). Using wives and concubines as the connecting thread, it yokes the current regime to the age of the early, legendary Abbasids.

Today most of Ibn al-Sāʿī's prolific and varied output is lost, although much of it was extant as late as the eleventh/seventeenth century[18] and scattered quotations survive in other authors. Scholars disagree whether *Brief Lives* is really by Ibn al-Sāʿī, probably because, unlike *Consorts of the Caliphs* and the *Concise Summation of Representative and Outstanding Historical and Biographical Events*, the only other surviving work indisputably attributed to him,[19] it has no scholarly apparatus.[20] But it is certainly the work of *a* Baghdadi survivor of the Mongol sack, typical of a period which produced quantities of histories of all kinds (as did Ibn al-Sāʿī himself).[21] As for Ibn al-Sāʿī, he was sixty-three when Baghdad fell. Outwardly, little changed for him in the eighteen years he still had to live: his career as a librarian continued uninterrupted.[22] Perhaps the real cultural rift had occurred before the arrival of the Mongols. The supposedly happy and glorious reign of al-Nāṣir li-Dīn Allāh, "Champion of the Faith," in which Ibn al-Sāʿī was born, was unprecedentedly totalitarian: according to one contemporary, the caliph's spies were so efficient and the caliph himself so ruthless that a man hardly dared speak to his own wife in the privacy of his home.[23] Courtly life centered on al-Nāṣir as the teacher of true doctrine and keystone of social cohesion.[24] The latter-day ladies of the caliph's household showcased by Ibn al-Sāʿī in *Consorts of the Caliphs* partake, in his eyes, of this godly ethos, and are public figures with political clout. On the face of it, they have nothing in common with the vulnerable aesthetes whose hothouse loves and whose music, poetry, and wit set their stamp on the early Abbasid court, and who are given far more space in *Consorts of the Caliphs*.[25] These figures so fascinate Ibn al-Sāʿī that he stretches his book's brief to include a life sketch of one, the famous poet ʿInān, who may not have been a caliph's concubine.[26]

Consorts of the Caliphs as Abbasid Loyalism

Why was Ibn al-Sāʿī so interested in Abbasid caliphs' wives and lovers? Why was he equally committed to the aesthetes and to the doers of good works? There are two answers. The first is that he was a fervent loyalist. About one third of all the writings ascribed to him were devoted to the Abbasids. Of the nineteen such titles listed by Muṣṭafā Jawād in the introduction to his 1962 edition of *Consorts of the Caliphs*, under the title *Jihāt al-aʾimmah al-khulafāʾ min al-ḥarāʾir wa-l-imāʾ*, the following were clearly designed to please, and as propaganda for, current members of the ruling house: *Cognizance of the Virtues of the Caliphs of the House of al-ʿAbbās* (*al-Īnās bi-manāqib al-khulafāʾ min Banī l-ʿAbbās*);[27] *The Flower-Filled Garden: Episodes from the Life of the Caliph al-Nāṣir* (*al-Rawḍ al-nāḍir fī akhbār al-imām al-Nāṣir*),[28] along with a life of a slave of al-Nāṣir, his commander-in-chief, Qushtimir (*Nuzhat al-rāghib al-muʿtabir fī sīrat al-malik Qushtimir*);[29] a life of the caliph al-Mustanṣir (*Iʿtibār al-mustabṣir fī sīrat al-Mustanṣir*) and a collection of poems—"ropes of pearls"—in his praise, most likely composed by Ibn al-Sāʿī himself (*al-Qalāʾid al-durriyyah fī l-madāʾiḥ al-Mustanṣiriyyah*);[30] a life of the caliph al-Mustaʿṣim (*Sīrat al-Mustaʿṣim bi-llāh*); and a book "about the blessed al-Mustaʿṣim's two sons: how much was spent on them, details of their food and clothing, and the poems written in their praise" (*Nuzhat al-abṣār fī akhbār ibnay al-Mustaʿṣim bi-llāh al-ʿAbbāsī*).[31]

The caliphs were active in endowing libraries: al-Nāṣir that of the old Niẓāmiyyah Law College as well as that of the Sufi convent (*ribāṭ*) founded by his wife Saljūqī Khātūn,[32] al-Mustanṣir that of the law college he had founded in 631/1233–34, the Mustanṣiriyyah. For grandees to add their own gifts of books was a way of ingratiating themselves with the ruler.[33] Ibn al-Sāʿī was a librarian in both colleges, before and after the Mongol invasion, as already mentioned,[34] so the following titles should be counted as part of his loyalist output: *The High Virtues of the Teachers of the Niẓāmiyyah Law College* (*al-Manāqib al-ʿaliyyah li-mudarrisī l-madrasah al-Niẓāmiyyah*) and *The Regulations of the Mustanṣiriyyah Law College* (*Sharṭ al-madrasah al-Mustanṣiriyyah*).[35]

How do the early Abbasid concubines of *Consorts of the Caliphs* fit into this program of glorifying the dynasty's virtues? The first entries on them describe only their subjects' physical and intellectual qualities. But about halfway through the book comes a pivotal entry, that on Isḥāq al-Andalusiyyah, concubine of al-Mutawakkil and mother of his son, the great regent al-Muwaffaq. When she died in 270/883, during the regency, a court poet composed a majestic elegy on her, describing her public benefactions and her private, maternal virtues, which were also public in that her son was the savior of the state.[36] Ibn al-Sāʿī lets the poem speak for itself, but the reader might be expected to know that al-Muwaffaq had been engaged for years in putting down a rebellion of black plantation slaves in lower Iraq, which had caused widespread damage and panic. He finally crushed it in the year of his mother's death.[37] Contemporary loyalist readers would certainly have made a connection between this tribute to the virtuous mother of a heroic son and the elegies collected by Ibn al-Sāʿī on "the blessed consort, Lady Zumurrud," mother of the caliph al-Nāṣir li-Dīn Allāh (*Marāthī al-jihah al-saʿīdah Zumurrud Khātūn wālidat al-khalīfah al-Nāṣir li-Dīn Allāh*).[38]

As *Consorts of the Caliphs* progresses, the theme of feminine virtue becomes more frequent. Thus Maḥbūbah, the slave of al-Mutawakkil, mourns him defiantly after his murder, at the risk of her life, and dies of grief for him.[39] Ḍirār, concubine of the regent al-Muwaffaq and mother of his son, the caliph al-Muʿtaḍid, another great ruler, was "always mindful of her dependents."[40] The princess Qaṭr al-Nadā, wife of al-Muʿtaḍid, was "one of the most intelligent and regal women who ever lived"—sufficiently so to puncture the caliph's arrogance.[41] Khamrah, slave of the murdered caliph al-Muqtadir (son of al-Muʿtaḍid) and mother of al-Muqtadir's son Prince ʿĪsā, "was always mindful of her obligations and performed many pious deeds. She was generous to the poor, to the needy, to those who petitioned her, and to noble families who had fallen on hard times"[42]—the kind of encomium that Ibn al-Sāʿī goes on to apply to late-Abbasid consorts. Khamrah ends the sequence of early-Abbasid concubines; after her begins a series of virtuous Saljūq princesses and late-Abbasid models of female virtue whose merits clearly redound to the honor of the dynasty as a whole—merits which in Ibn al-Sāʿī's time, at least before the Mongols, were highly visible in the streetscape of Baghdad, in the shape of the public works and mausolea ordered by these women.[43] In this, important ladies of the caliph's household were following the example of Zubaydah, the most famous of early-Abbasid princesses, well-known to every citizen of Baghdad and indeed to every pilgrim to Mecca,[44] and Ibn al-Sāʿī, in recording their piety, good works, and burial places, is following the example of his older contemporary, Ibn al-Jawzī.[45] According to Jawād, Ibn al-Sāʿī means "Son of the Runner" or merchant's errand-man; if it is not a surname taken from a distant ancestor, but instead reflects a humble background—as Jawād argues, on the basis that Ibn al-Sāʿī's father Anjab is unknown to biographers[46]—then Ibn al-Sāʿī's grateful descriptions of the later consorts' public works may reflect the feelings of ordinary Baghdadis.

Virtue, however—loyalty or piety-based virtue that finds social expression—is not the whole reason why Ibn al-Sāʿī devotes so much space to the early-Abbasid concubines, since most of them are not virtuous at all by these standards.

The Early-Abbasid Consorts as Culture Heroines

The majority of the early-Abbasid consorts were professional poets and musicians. Ibn al-Sāʿī and his sources, which include nearly all the great names in mid-Abbasid cultural mythography,[47] rate them very highly: ʿInān "was the first poet to become famous under the Abbasids and the most gifted poet of her generation"; the major (male) poets of her time came to her to be judged.[48] No one "sang, played music, wrote poetry, or played chess so well" as ʿArīb.[49] Faḍl al-Shāʿirah was not only one of the greatest wits of her time, but wrote better prose than any state secretary.[50] Above all, they excel in the difficult art of capping verse and composing on the spur of the moment.[51] Their accomplishments are essentially competitive, and it is usually men that they compete with. The competition is not only a salon game. For the male poets—free men who make their living by performing at court—losing poses a risk to their reputation and livelihood. The women who challenge them or respond to their challenge are all slaves (*jāriyah* is the term used for such highly trained slave women). Of the risks to a slave woman who fails to perform, or to best her challenger, only one is spelled out in *Consorts of the Caliphs*, in the case of ʿInān, whose owner whips her.[52] On the other hand, the returns on talent and self-confidence can be great, as is seen in the case of ʿArīb, whose career continues into old age, when her verve and authority seem undiminished and she has apparently achieved a wealthy independence.[53] We are shown how, between poets, the fellowship of professionalism transcends differences between male and female, free and slave. But even in the battles of wits between a *jāriyah* and her lover, where the stakes are very high—if she misses her step, the woman risks not just the loss of favor and position, but the loss of affection too, for many *jāriyah*s are depicted as being truly in love with their owners—there is often, again, a touch of something like comradeship: a woman's ability to rise to the occasion can compel her lover's quasi-professional admiration. We should remember that nearly all the early-Abbasid caliphs composed poetry or music themselves, and they all considered themselves highly competent judges. Though the consorts' beauty is routinely mentioned, when we are shown a cause of attraction, it is the cleverness, aptness, or pathos of their poetry that wins over the lover. The workings of attraction and esteem can be imagined and explored in the case of slaves as they rarely are in that of free women; and this, in addition to their talents and exquisite sensibility or dashing manners, is what makes the early-Abbasid *jāriyah*s culture heroines, whose hold on the Arabic imagination persists through the ages.

Ibn al-Sāʿī's Contribution

Unlike Abū l-Faraj al-Iṣfahānī, the authority most cited in *Consorts of the Caliphs*,[54] Ibn al-Sāʿī seems far less interested in music than in poetry. He was a poet himself, as indeed was almost any contemporary Arabic speaker with any claim to literacy and social competence. He and all his readers knew the wide range of available poetic genres, both ceremonial and intimate. As children, they would have been taught the ancient and modern Arabic poetic classics, and as adults, they might have written verse on public occasions and would certainly have composed poems to entertain their friends, lampoon unpleasant colleagues, or give vent to their feelings about life. The poetry of the *jāriyah*s has its own place in this spectrum. It is occasional poetry: even when they write accession panegyrics or congratulations on a successful military campaign, the *jāriyah*s keep them short and light.[55] What is poignant about their poetry is its ephemerality: it captures and belongs to the moment. And what is especially moving about it is that (in the eyes of Ibn al-Sāʿī, who simplifes but does not traduce the complex vision of Abū l-Faraj al-Iṣfahānī) it is identical with the woman who composes it and her precarious situation. As Ibn al-Sāʿī tells it, the poetry of the slave consorts is an act of personal daring and moral agency, which finds its reward in the love of the caliph and sometimes even in marriage.[56] This is something considerable, contained in the small compass of the anecdote format.

There have not been many attempts, in modern scholarship, to make distinctions between the *jāriyah*s as poets and cultural agents, on the one hand, and as romantic heroines and objects of erotic and ethical fantasy, on the other. There are basic surveys of the sources;[57] there is a pioneering study of the world of Abū l-Faraj al-Iṣfahānī's *Book of Songs*;[58] and, most recently, there is an exploration of the values underlying the competition between *jāriyah*s and free male poets and musicians.[59] Medieval contemporaries were alive to the social paradox of the woman slave performer as a leader of fashion but also a commodity, an extravagance but also an investment for her owners, able to some extent to turn her status as a chattel to her own profit by manipulating her clients—and they satirized it unsympathetically.[60] By comparison, modern reflection on female slavery and its place in medieval Islamic societies is unsophisticated.[61] The time span of *Consorts of the Caliphs* is wider than that of the mid-Abbasid classics which have been the focus of modern scholarship until now, and the life stories it presents of female slaves bring together a greater range of backgrounds and situations and open up more complex perspectives.

Ibn al-Sāʿī's special contribution to the subject is his seriousness and sympathy, the multiplicity of roles within the dynasty that he identifies for consorts, and his systematic, and challenging, idealization of the woman over the slave.

Julia Bray

Maps

1. The Abbasid Caliphate
2. Early Baghdad
3. Later Baghdad
4. Later East Baghdad

Note: The maps of Baghdad are based principally on Le Strange, *Baghdad* (1900), Jawād and Sūsah, *Dalīl* (1958), Makdisi, "Topography" (1959), Lassner, *Topography* (1970), and Ahola and Osti, "Baghdad." In cases where precise locations are not known, the aim has been to give readers of *Consorts* an idea of the relationships between different places topographically. Outright conjectures are followed by a question mark.

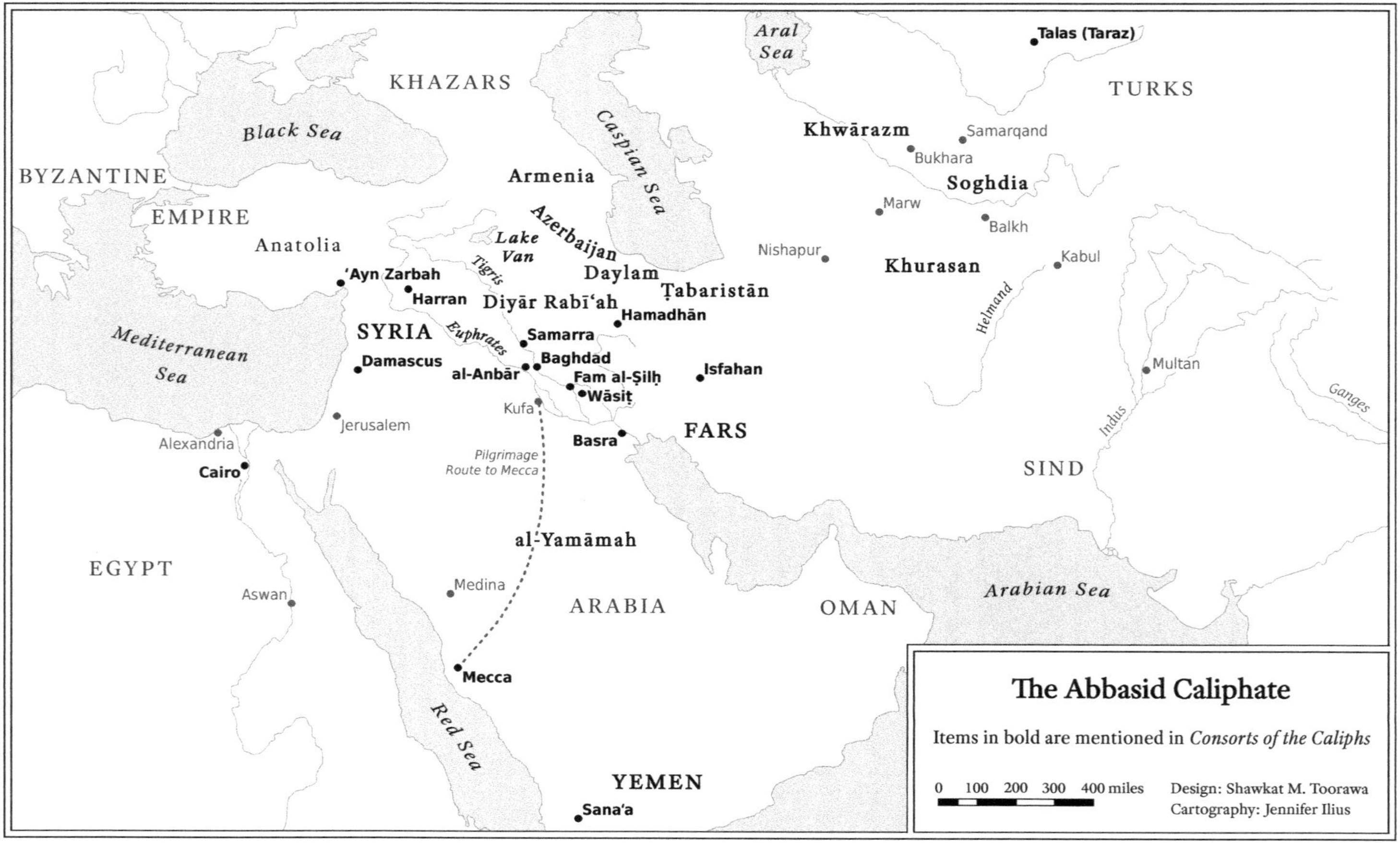
The Abbasid Caliphate
Items in bold are mentioned in Consorts of the Caliphs
0 100 200 300 400 miles
Design: Shawkat M. Toorawa
Cartography: Jennifer Ilius
Aral Sea
Talas (Taraz)
TURKS
KHAZARS
Black Sea
Caspian Sea
Khwārazm
Samarqand
Bukhara
Soghdia
BYZANTINE EMPIRE
Armenia
Marw
Balkh
Anatolia
Lake Van
Azerbaijan
Nishapur
Khurasan
Kabul
ʿAyn Zarbah
Tigris
Daylam
Ṭabaristān
Harran
Diyār Rabīʿah
Hamadhān
Helmand
SYRIA
Euphrates
Samarra
Mediterranean Sea
Baghdad
Damascus
al-Anbār
Fam al-Ṣilḥ
Wāsiṭ
Isfahan
Multan
Ganges
Kufa
Jerusalem
Alexandria
Basra
FARS
Indus
Pilgrimage Route to Mecca
Cairo
SIND
al-Yamāmah
EGYPT
Aswan
Medina
ARABIA
OMAN
Arabian Sea
Mecca
Red Sea
YEMEN
Sana'a

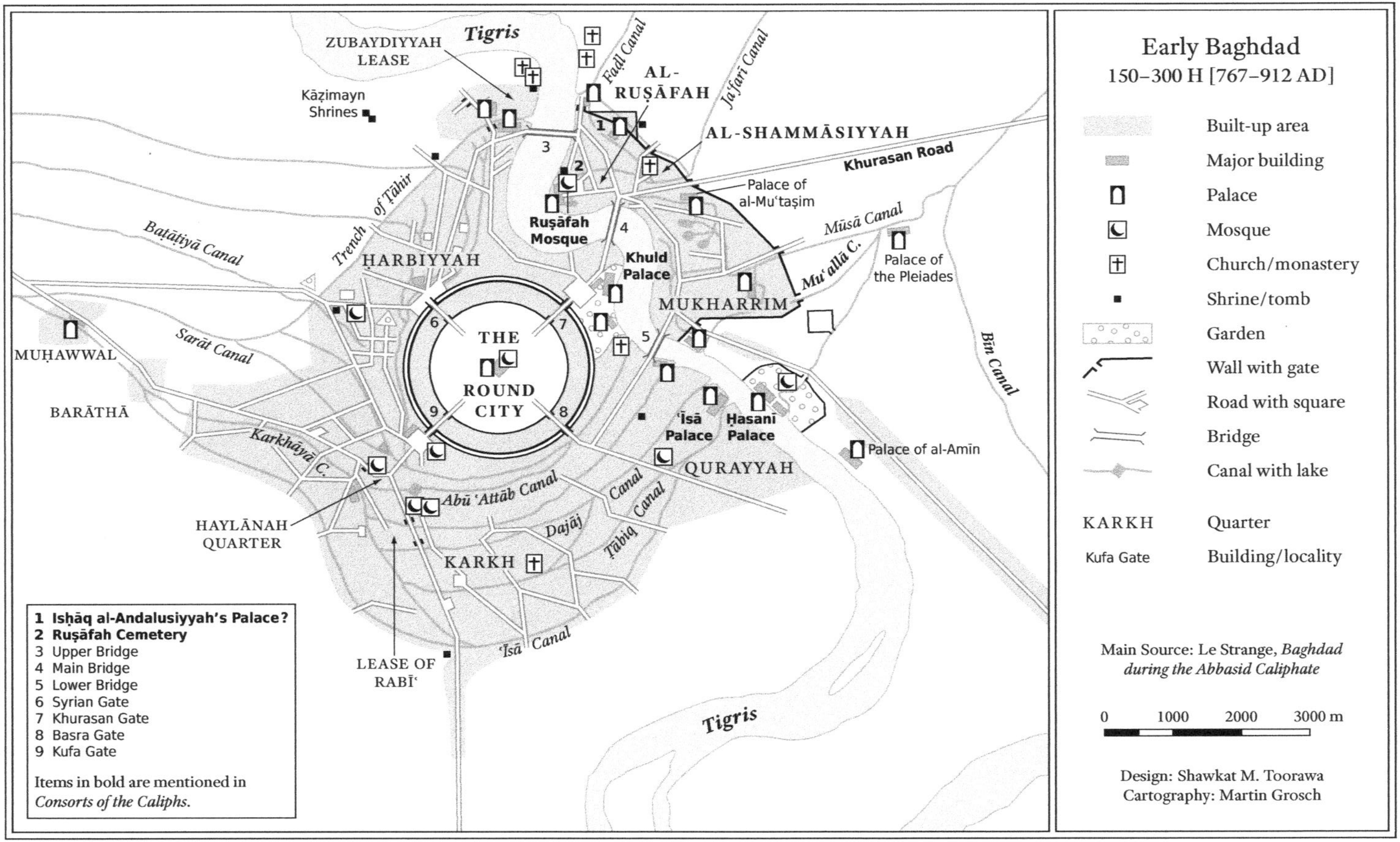
Early Baghdad
150–300 H [767–912 AD]
Built-up area
Major building
Palace
Mosque
Church/monastery
Shrine/tomb
Garden
Wall with gate
Road with square
Bridge
Canal with lake
KARKH
Quarter
Kufa Gate
Building/locality
Main Source: Le Strange, *Baghdad during the Abbasid Caliphate*
0
1000
2000
3000 m
Design: Shawkat M. Toorawa
Cartography: Martin Grosch
Tigris
ZUBAYDIYYAH LEASE
Kāẓimayn Shrines
Faḍl Canal
AL-RUṢĀFAH
Ja'farī Canal
AL-SHAMMĀSIYYAH
Khurasan Road
Palace of al-Mu'taṣim
Ruṣāfah Mosque
Mūsā Canal
Mu'allā C.
Palace of the Pleiades
Khuld Palace
MUKHARRIM
Bīn Canal
Baṭāṭiyā Canal
Trench of Ṭāhir
ḤARBIYYAH
THE ROUND CITY
MUḤAWWAL
Ṣarāt Canal
BARĀTHĀ
Karkhāyā C.
'Īsā Palace
Ḥasanī Palace
Palace of al-Amīn
QURAYYAH
Abū 'Attāb Canal
Canal
Ṭābiq Canal
Dajāj
HAYLĀNAH QUARTER
KARKH
'Īsā Canal
LEASE OF RABĪ'
Tigris
1 Isḥāq al-Andalusiyyah's Palace?
2 Ruṣāfah Cemetery
3 Upper Bridge
4 Main Bridge
5 Lower Bridge
6 Syrian Gate
7 Khurasan Gate
8 Basra Gate
9 Kufa Gate
Items in bold are mentioned in *Consorts of the Caliphs*.

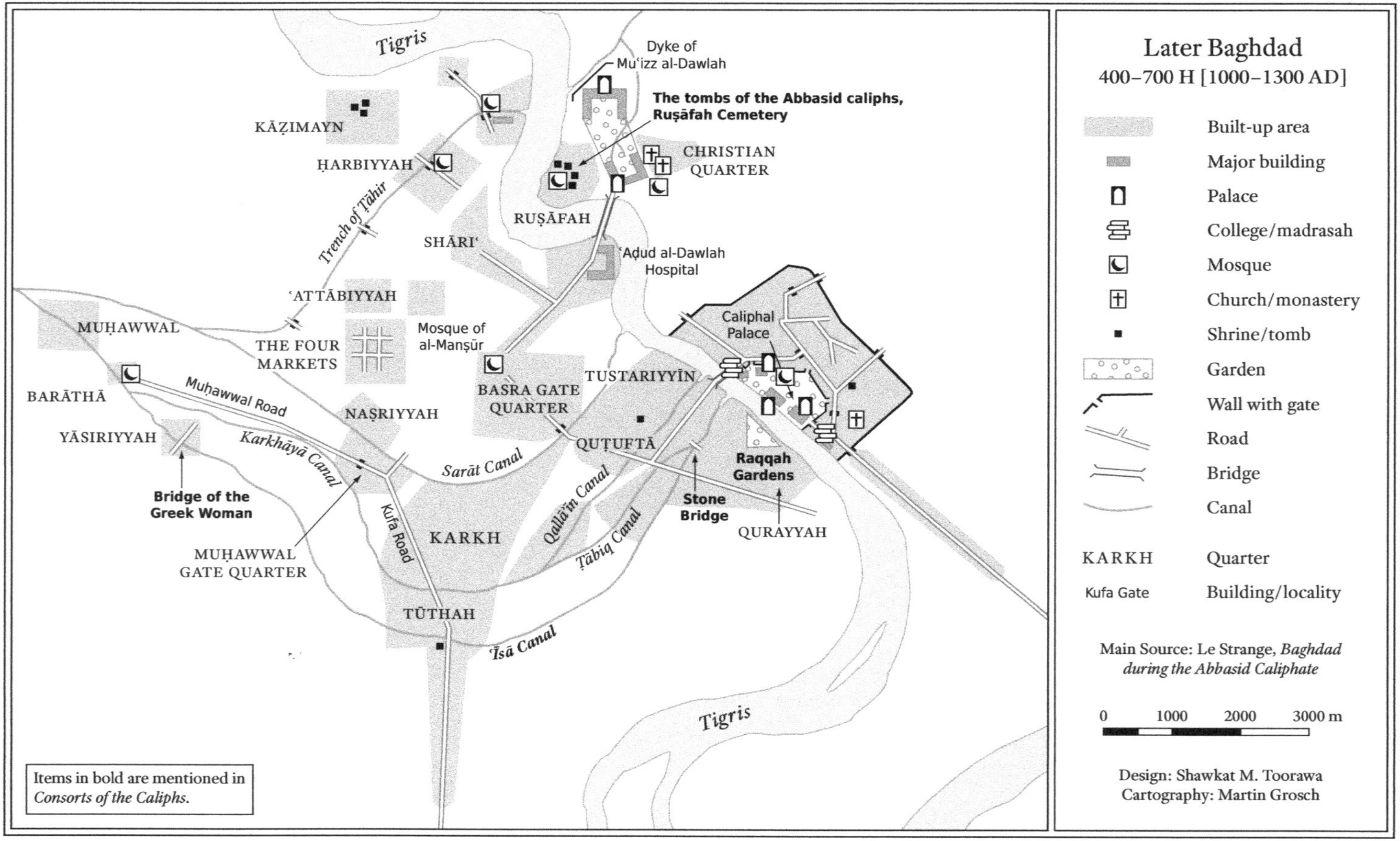

Later Baghdad
400–700 H [1000–1300 AD]
Built-up area
Major building
Palace
College/madrasah
Mosque
Church/monastery
Shrine/tomb
Garden
Wall with gate
Road
Bridge
Canal
KARKH
Quarter
Kufa Gate
Building/locality
Main Source: Le Strange, *Baghdad during the Abbasid Caliphate*
0 1000 2000 3000 m
Design: Shawkat M. Toorawa
Cartography: Martin Grosch
Tigris
Dyke of Mu'izz al-Dawlah
The tombs of the Abbasid caliphs, Ruṣāfah Cemetery
KĀẒIMAYN
ḤARBIYYAH
CHRISTIAN QUARTER
RUṢĀFAH
Trench of Ṭāhir
SHĀRI'
'Aḍud al-Dawlah Hospital
'ATTĀBIYYAH
MUḤAWWAL
THE FOUR MARKETS
Mosque of al-Manṣūr
Caliphal Palace
TUSTARIYYĪN
BARĀTHĀ
Muḥawwal Road
BASRA GATE QUARTER
NAṢRIYYAH
YĀSIRIYYAH
Karkhāyā Canal
QUṬUFTĀ
Sarāt Canal
Raqqah Gardens
Bridge of the Greek Woman
Kufa Road
Qallā'īn Canal
Stone Bridge
KARKH
Ṭābiq Canal
QURAYYAH
MUḤAWWAL GATE QUARTER
TŪTHAH
'Īsā Canal
Tigris
Items in bold are mentioned in *Consorts of the Caliphs*.

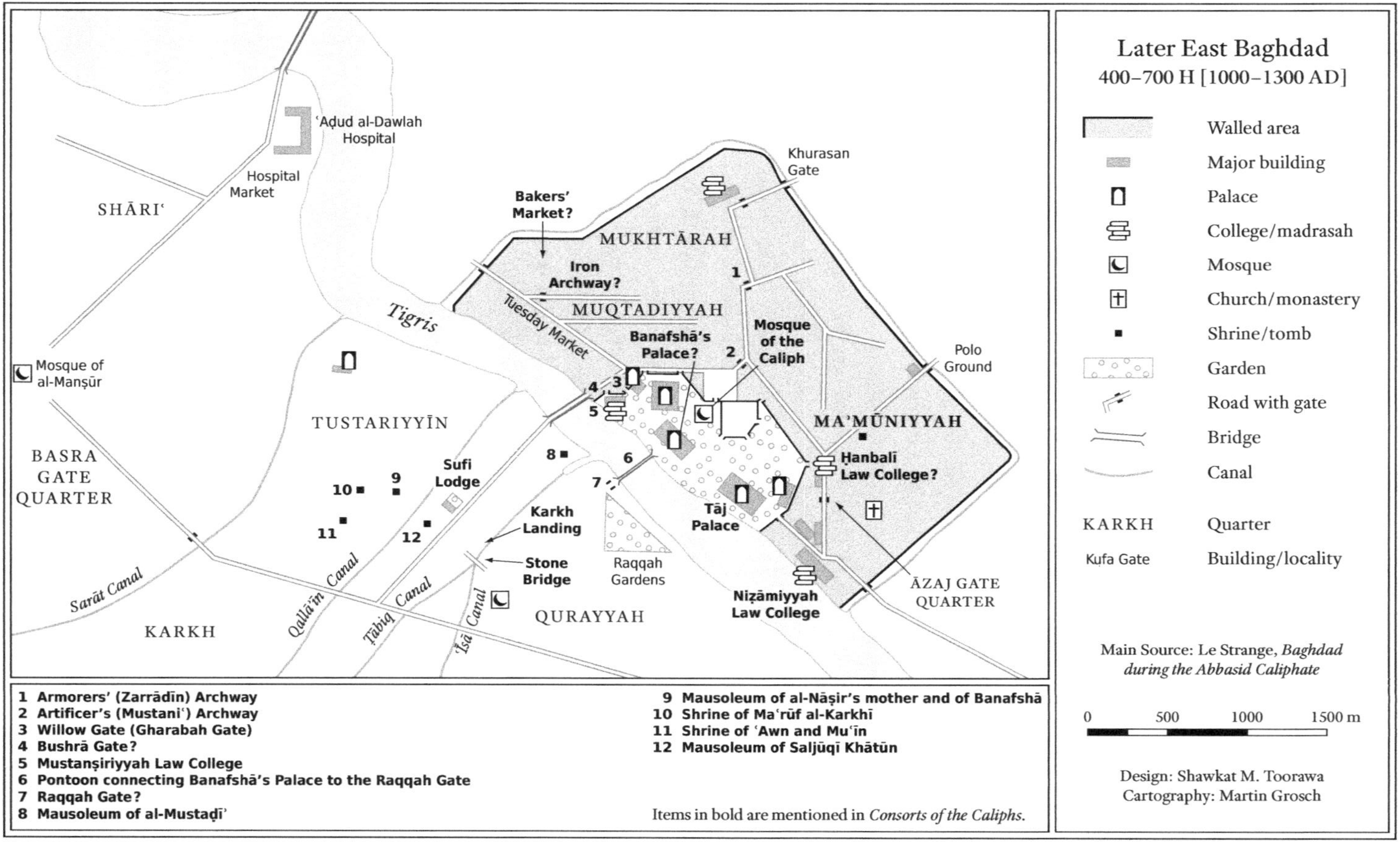

Later East Baghdad
400–700 H [1000–1300 AD]
Walled area
Major building
Palace
College/madrasah
Mosque
Church/monastery
Shrine/tomb
Garden
Road with gate
Bridge
Canal
KARKH
Quarter
Kufa Gate
Building/locality
Main Source: Le Strange, *Baghdad during the Abbasid Caliphate*
0
500
1000
1500 m
Design: Shawkat M. Toorawa
Cartography: Martin Grosch
ʿAḍud al-Dawlah Hospital
Hospital Market
SHĀRIʿ
Mosque of al-Manṣūr
BASRA GATE QUARTER
TUSTARIYYĪN
KARKH
Tigris
Sarāt Canal
Qallāʾīn Canal
Ṭābiq Canal
ʿĪsā Canal
Sufi Lodge
Karkh Landing
Stone Bridge
Raqqah Gardens
QURAYYAH
Bakers' Market?
Iron Archway?
MUKHTĀRAH
MUQTADIYYAH
Tuesday Market
Banafshā's Palace?
Mosque of the Caliph
Khurasan Gate
Polo Ground
MAʾMŪNIYYAH
Ḥanbalī Law College?
Tāj Palace
Niẓāmiyyah Law College
ĀZAJ GATE QUARTER
1
2
3
4
5
6
7
8
9
10
11
12
1 Armorers' (Zarrādīn) Archway
2 Artificer's (Mustaniʿ) Archway
3 Willow Gate (Gharabah Gate)
4 Bushrā Gate?
5 Mustanṣiriyyah Law College
6 Pontoon connecting Banafshā's Palace to the Raqqah Gate
7 Raqqah Gate?
8 Mausoleum of al-Mustaḍīʾ
9 Mausoleum of al-Nāṣir's mother and of Banafshā
10 Shrine of Maʿrūf al-Karkhī
11 Shrine of ʿAwn and Muʿīn
12 Mausoleum of Saljūqī Khātūn
Items in bold are mentioned in *Consorts of the Caliphs*.

Note on the Translation

SHAWKAT M. TOORAWA

The project of translating Ibn al-Sāʿī's *Consorts of the Caliphs* was first suggested by Joseph Lowry to the academic alliance Radical Reassessment of Arabic Arts, Language, and Literature (RRAALL), of which he and three other Library of Arabic Literature editors are members—Michael Cooperson, Devin Stewart, and myself, Shawkat Toorawa.[62] Having successfully published a collaboratively authored book on Arabic autobiography in 2001,[63] RRAALL was looking for a follow-up project. Lowry made the case that *Consorts of the Caliphs* captured our various and varied interests (the Abbasids, art and archaeology, ethnomusicology, gender, history, language, law, literature, the Saljūqs), that it was short, that it was divided into manageable parts, and that it was of inherent interest.[64] By 2008, eight of us had translated consecutive portions and we had a complete if uneven working translation. In 2009, Lowry, Stewart, and I met in Philadelphia to even out the translation and subsequently dispatched it to Cooperson, who made many changes and suggestions. Then the project went quiet.

In 2009, when Philip Kennedy asked me what kinds of works I thought one might include in a "library of Arabic literature"—then still only an idea—I mentioned, among other works, Ibn al-Sāʿī's little book. I even told him a "draft translation" was available. Later, when the Library of Arabic Literature (LAL) had become a reality, Kennedy (now the LAL's General Editor), who hadn't forgotten Ibn al-Sāʿī, mentioned the book to the board. In 2011, Julia Bray suggested that it was an ideal candidate for a collaborative LAL project and so, one morning in New York City, we resolved to take it on, with the blessings of RRAALL and of the LAL board. We realized—as we had been realizing and discovering with other LAL books that we had already edited—that the "draft translation," in spite of the effort that had been put into it, was less a translation than it was an "Englished" version of the Arabic, in a prose that we have come to think of unflatteringly as "industry standard."

Process

Our first act was to appoint a project editor from our own LAL editorial board, as we do with all our projects. We chose Julia Bray, who went through the "draft translation" and wrote a report describing what needed to be done to bring it up to LAL standard—something we require for all potential LAL projects. At the same time, we showed it to the distinguished translator Richard Sieburth. With Bray's and Sieburth's positive but critical feedback, we decided that it was best to start from scratch. We divided the book into five parts and assigned each part to a team of two; the ten people involved were the eight LAL board members, the managing editor, and Richard Sieburth. After our first workshop we presented our preliminary thoughts and samples of our work at a public event in Abu Dhabi. For the next workshop, we invited Justin Stearns and Maurice Pomerantz (both of New York University Abu Dhabi) to join us and we shuffled around the teams. After these teams had done their translations and conferred among themselves and with one another, I then collated their material, made the various parts consistent based on the principles and choices that we had agreed upon, and e-mailed the material to everyone to read through and ponder.

We held a final workshop during our May 2014 editorial meeting in New York City, where we projected the translation onto a screen and went through it all together, comparing it to the manuscript. At the end of three half-day sessions, we had thrashed out many issues, which involved, among other things, reversing course on certain key decisions. Then, in a final daylong session, Julia Bray (the designated project editor) and I (the designated editor of the book) spent a most genial day going through it all again line by line, establishing new principles, establishing consistency where it was not yet present, and deciding on shape and format. Julia then returned to Oxford and I to Ithaca.

I then went through the entire translation again, implementing all of our decisions, and when I was satisfied I sent it back to Julia Bray to vet carefully. I also sent it to Joseph Lowry for his feedback. After I had incorporated Joe's feedback and intervened stylistically again myself, we sent the translation to Marina Warner, who very graciously agreed to write a foreword. Julia then sent me further detailed comments and annotations, which I addressed and incorporated, and she proceeded to write her introduction.

At that point, I set about producing fuller notes to the translation. I also prepared preliminary glossaries. LAL policy is to have one unified glossary of names, places, and terms, but in this case we felt that separate glossaries of the authorities (authors and transmitters cited) and the characters featured in the anecdotes, of place names, and of realia would be far more useful to reader and scholar alike; we also decided that we would gloss every individual in the book. As I finished each constituent part, I sent it to Julia, who went over it very carefully. We would often catch a problem, or discover a reference that we wanted to insert, on our third or fourth exchange or read-through.

Once everything—front matter, Arabic edition and notes, English translation and notes, glossaries, indices—was ready, I sent it all off to Julia, in her capacity as project editor, so that she could vet it one last time and make any final crucial interventions. Once she gave the go-ahead, an executive editor—in this case James Montgomery, who made numerous valuable suggestions—did an executive review and then gave the green light to our managing editor, Chip Rossetti, to put the book into production.

The reason I have given such a detailed description of the process is that I want to highlight the fact that this is in every way a collaborative translation, and has been from the very beginning. It is true that in the final stages, Julia and I ended up making many decisions without the input of the rest of the group, but these were generally very small and/or stylistic decisions or else instances where we realized we had misinterpreted and therefore mistranslated something. Macro-level decisions were always taken as a group, after protracted discussion. As for the front and back matter, Julia and I collaborated extensively. And as I have described above, Joseph Lowry and James Montgomery had the opportunity to weigh in again.

Principles

The first and easily most important question we faced was whether and how to translate names, designations, and titles. The second entry in the collection, for example, is devoted to "Ghādir jāriyat al-Imām al-Hādī." "Ghādir" is a nickname or pet name meaning "treacherous" or "inconstant." We could not initially agree whether to render the name in English or keep it in Arabic. Not to translate a nickname would be to shortchange the English reader; she could, it is true, learn from a footnote what a name means, but she might miss the fact that the name means what it means every time it is used. The group also agreed, however, that the "meaning" might constitute an undue distraction and sound odd besides. There are names that are meaningful but which one might not wish to translate; imagine a Spanish text featuring a woman named Concepción—one would likely not translate her name into the English "Conception." We eventually decided to use Arabic names throughout. In the case of slaves, we provide a translation in quotation marks after the first occurrence (as it happens, typically in the heading), but use the Arabic name thereafter. In the case of the freeborn, however, we do not translate the name.

This decision extended to the titles of caliphs. The choice of a regnal title, whether made by the caliph himself or bestowed on him as heir apparent, was always significant and sometimes reflected a program; such is the case for al-Nāṣir li-Dīn Allāh (husband of Saljūqī Khātūn, no. 29 below), who aspired to be "The Champion of the Faith," but even though Arabic readers will be very aware of the meanings of such titles, it is not the norm to translate them. As for the title *Imām* preceding a caliph's name, that is one standard way of referring to a caliph, but it was clear to us that to use the title "Imam" in English would cause confusion, whereas to use "Caliph," as we have, would be unambiguous. We also decided that the caliphal title "Amīr al-Mu'minīn," literally "Commander of the Faithful" and routinely used as a form of address, could sound clumsy in some contexts in English; we opted instead for "Sire" or "My lord" in many, though not all, cases.

The word *jāriyah* in the phrase "Ghādir jāriyat al-Imām al-Hādī" is often translated "slave girl" or "singing-girl." While some of us thought that the demeaning aspect of the word "girl" was a positive feature of the word in this case, appropriate for describing someone who was a slave, no matter how accomplished or respected, others of us thought it would be more powerful (if that is the right word) to use "female slave" or "slave"—and this view prevailed. In the end, we settled on "slave" alone. The Ghādir heading thus reads:

Ghādir
"Inconstance"
Slave of the Caliph al-Hādī

As for the English rendering of the names of characters and transmitters in the text, we occasionally shorten long genealogies to make them less unwieldy for English readers. Names of well-known figures that appear in the text in a form unfamiliar to modern readers (which is usually an indication of how familiar Ibn al-Sāʿī himself was with them) are identified in the glossary.

Other decisions we made about the translation include the following:

- With a few exceptions (typically in the case of well-known figures or long genealogies), we render names the way they appear in the Arabic on first occurrence and thereafter shorten them to a standard form, e.g. Abū l-Faraj al-Iṣfahānī, al-Ṭabarī, or Thābit ibn Sinān.
- We only translate a professional designation—e.g. "the trustee 'Abd al-Wahhāb ibn 'Alī"—when we are confident that it was the profession of the individual in question, rather than the equivalent of a modern surname.
- We follow the spelling conventions of the *Encyclopaedia of Islam, Three.*
- We render Saljūq names in Arabicized forms.
- In the longer *isnād*s—the succession or "chain" of transmitters of an anecdote or other item of information—we frequently use long dashes to separate the sources that intervene between Ibn al-Sāʿī's own informant and the original source of the information, so as to make it easier for the reader to follow the transmission.
- We routinely substitute pronouns for proper names to make the meaning clearer. Occasionally we do the opposite, expanding a pronoun, to make attribution clearer to the reader; thus in §8.8.3, where the Arabic has simply "He said that," we render it "Here our source, Abū l-ʿAynāʾ, notes . . ."
- Because we use "Isfahan" for the city, we use "al-Iṣfahānī" for the name (even though we have retained the predominating "Iṣbahān" and "al-Iṣbahānī" in the Arabic, as explained in the "Note on the Edition" above).
- We have striven to make the poetry rhyme when the context or verse itself required it and used devices such as half-rhyme or assonance when the meaning of the verse or anecdote depended on it. When forcing a poem to rhyme in English

would have meant altering the original meaning, we have not done so.

- Translations from the Qur'an are our own.

Note also:

- Though many anecdotes in *Consorts of the Caliphs* appear in other extant works, we do not provide cross-references (these are available in Jawād's edition).
- We italicize the poetry to make it stand out from the rest of the text.
- The maps of Baghdad in some cases do not so much reflect precise locations as they do the topographical relationships between different locations.
- The first three glossaries—of characters; of authorities (authors and transmitters); and of places—contain all the names that occur in *Consorts of the Caliphs*. We also provide a fourth glossary, of realia.

In 2010, when we first told colleagues how LAL would work—numerous stages and levels of close editorial scrutiny, the assigning of in-house project editors to each and every volume, master classes in editing and translating, and collaborative, workshopped translations—most, if not all, were skeptical. We hope that this volume, which was produced according to these principles and norms, will help alleviate any doubts about the possibility, viability, and desirability of such an enterprise, and that it will come to be seen as one model for how things can be done and—such is our hope—done well.

Shawkat M. Toorawa, *on behalf of the translators*

Notes to the Front Matter

Foreword

1 Ardener, "Belief and the Problem of Women" and "The Problem Revisited."

2 See Ibn al-Sāʿī, *Consorts of the Caliphs*, §13.5 below. References to *Consorts of the Caliphs* are hereafter referred to by the paragraph number of the entry.

Preface

3 Details of how we workshopped and translated the book can be found in the "Note on the Translation" below.

Introduction

4 Jawād, "Introduction," 18, 20, in Ibn al-Sāʿī, *Nisāʾ al-khulafāʾ*.

5 The "daughter of Ṭulūn the Turk" "who married one of her dalliances" (§35).

6 See §30.5 and §§31–39 below.

7 See §10.2 and §16.2, where impressive *isnād*s serve in each case to introduce a two-line occasional poem.

8 See §30.4.1.

9 See "Note on the Edition" in the hardcover edition of Consorts of the Caliphs.

10 See "Note on the Translation" below; for the text of the miscellany, see the "Online Material > Book Supplements" page of the website of the Library of Arabic Literature: www.libraryofarabicliterature.org.

11 Ibn al-Sāʿī, *Mukhtaṣar*, 142.

12 See Hartmann, "al-Nāṣir li-Dīn Allāh"; and Hillenbrand, "al-Mustanṣir (I)."

13 Ibn al-Sāʿī, *Mukhtaṣar*, 127.

14 *Brief Lives* adopts this inaccurate periodicity for dramatic effect. In *Consorts of the Caliphs*, the following are mentioned as having been killed: the sixth Abbasid caliph, al-Amīn (r. 193–98/809–13) (at §11); the tenth, al-Mutawakkil (r. 232–47/847–61) (at §15.6); and the eighteenth, al-Muqtadir (r. 295–320/908–32) (at §23.1).

15 Ibn al-Sāʿī, *Mukhtaṣar*, 129–41.

16 See §30.4.1.

17 See §26 (Khātūn), §27 (Banafshā), §29 (Saljūqī Khātūn). ʿIṣmah Khātūn (§24) founded a law college in Isfahan; Shāhān (§30) spent huge sums on Baghdadi tradesmen, and Khātūn al-Safariyyah (§37) provisioned the pilgrim route.

18 Jawād's bibliography gives the titles of fifty-six items. Items 1–7, 9, 12, 15, 17–24, 26, 34–37, 39, 43–46, 51, 53 and 55 are listed by the Ottoman bibliographer Ḥājjī Khalīfah (1017–67/1609–57); see Jawād, "Introduction," 23–32, for references.

19 Ibn al-Sāʿī, *al-Jāmiʿ al-mukhtaṣar*. It originally went up to 1258, but of the original thirty volumes, only volume 9 (years 595–606/1199–1209) is extant; see Jawād, "Introduction," 26, no. 21.

20 Against the attribution are Jawād, "Introduction," 24, n. 4 and, seemingly, Lindsay, "Ibn al-Sāʿī." Rosenthal, "Ibn al-Sāʿī," 925, thinks it a "brief and mediocre history . . . unlikely to go back to [Ibn al-Sāʿī]." The attribution is silently accepted by Ziriklī, *al-Aʿlām*, 4:265, and Hartmann, "al-Nāṣir li-Dīn Allāh." Robinson, *Islamic Historiography*, 117, argues that it is an epitome composed by Ibn al-Sāʿī as part of "a large industry of popularizing history" that had been practiced for centuries.

21 Ibn al-Sāʿī wrote several histories of the caliphs, including one whose title suggests it was in verse: *Naẓm manthūr al-kalām fī dhikr al-khulafāʾ al-kirām* (*Versified Prose: the Noble Caliphs Recalled*). This

was presumably meant as an aide-mémoire, verse (*naẓm*) being more memorizable than prose (*manthūr al-kalām*). He wrote another "for persons of refinement" (*ẓurafā'*), *Bulghat al-ẓurafā' ilā ma'rifat tārīkh al-khulafā'* (*Getting to Know the History of the Caliphs, for Persons of Refinement*); see Jawād, "Introduction," 32, no. 53, and 25, no. 17. Another example of his practice of recasting his own works was his commentary on the famous and difficult literary *Maqāmāt* (fifty picaresque episodes in rhymed prose and verse) of al-Ḥarīrī (446–516/1054–1122), which he produced in three sizes: jumbo (twenty-five volumes), medium, and abridged; see Jawād, "Introduction," 32, no. 54, and 28, nos. 33 and 32.

22 Jawād, "Introduction," 16–17, 19.

23 Ibn Wāṣil al-Ḥamawī (604–97/1208–98), MS of *Ishfā' al-qulūb*, f. 231, quoted by Jawād, "Introduction," 8; see also Hartmann, "al-Nāṣir li-Dīn Allāh," 999, 1001.

24 Hartmann, "al-Nāṣir li-Dīn Allāh," 999–1002.

25 §§2–7, 9–11, 13–19, 31; see also 34, 36.

26 §3.2.

27 Jawād, "Introduction," 25, no. 15; see also 30, no. 47: *Manāqib al-khulafā' al-'Abbāsiyyīn* (*The Virtues of the Abbasid Caliphs*).

28 Jawād, "Introduction," 27, no. 27.

29 Jawād, "Introduction," 31, no. 52. Ibn al-Sā'ī refers to this work in the year 596/1199–1200 in *al-Jāmi' al-mukhtaṣar*, 9:43.

30 Jawād, "Introduction," 25, no. 12, and 29, no. 38.

31 Jawād, "Introduction," 28, no. 29, and 31, no. 50.

32 Jawād, "Introduction," 17, quoting al-Qifṭī (568–646/1172–1248), *Tārīḫ al-ḥukamā'*, 177. This seems to have been in addition to the library installed in Saljūqī Khātūn's mausoleum: see §29.2.1; and §29.2.2 for the Sufi lodge which according to Ibn al-Sā'ī was built not by Saljūqī Khātūn, but by al-Nāṣir in her memory.

33 See a later source that quotes Ibn al-Sā'ī as a witness to such donations, cited by Jawād, "Introduction," 21.

34 Jawād, "Introduction," 18, 20.

35 Jawād, "Introduction," 30, no. 48, and 28, no. 34.

36 §12.3.

37 On the Zanj rebellion, see Kennedy, *The Prophet and the Age of the Caliphates*, 180–81.

38 See Jawād, "Introduction," 29, no. 42. Zumurrud was a slave: see n. 100 in the main text below. She died in Jumada al-Thani, 599 [February, 1203], according to the sources quoted by Kaḥḥālah in his dictionary of notable women, *Aʿlām al-nisāʾ*, 2:39. Ibn al-Sāʿī records her death a month earlier, in Rabiʿ al-Thani, and quotes part of a long elegy by a court poet "which I have given in its entirety in *Elegies on the Blessed Consort Lady Zumurrud, Mother of the Caliph al-Nāṣir li-Dīn Allāh*," *al-Jāmiʿ al-mukhtaṣar*, 9:102, 279.

39 §15.6.

40 §21.1.

41 §22.1–2.

42 §23.3.

43 See the maps immediately following this introduction.

44 Zubaydah, the wife of Hārūn al-Rashīd, was famous for provisioning the pilgrim route with wells and resting places.

45 Under the caliph al-Muqtafī (530–55/1136–60), Abū l-Faraj ʿAbd al-Raḥmān ibn ʿAlī ibn al-Jawzī (ca. 511–97/1116–1201), head of two, then five, Baghdad madrasahs, enjoyed an "extraordinary career as a preacher . . . through his influence on the masses, he was politically important for those caliphs who, in their struggle with the military and the Saljūqs, followed a Ḥanbalī-Sunnī orientation. Diminishing influence under other caliphs was due to different policies adopted by them" (Seidensticker, "Ibn al-Jawzī," 338). In his history, *al-Muntaẓam fī tārīkh al-mulūk wa-l-umam*, (*The Well-Ordered History of Rulers and Nations*) "Ibn al-Jawzī . . . several times uses the obituary sections of his regnal annals to highlight the virtues of the mothers or consorts of caliphs. It seems likely that this device serves to redeem the reigns of caliphs who are not themselves wholly satisfactory from Ibn al-Jawzī's viewpoint, and that it is meant to suggest a continuity of virtue in the Abbasid caliphate as a political institution" (Bray, "A Caliph and His Public Relations," 36). Ibn al-Jawzī

records the funerals or burials of notables, especially women, in considerable detail; so too does Ibn al-Sāʿī in *Consorts of the Caliphs*: see §21.2, §22.3, §23.2, §24.1, §25.2, §27.4, §28.1, §29.2.1, §29.2.2, §29.3, §32.1 and §33.1. One of Ibn al-Sāʿī's works was devoted to cemeteries and shrines: *al-Maqābir al-mashhūrah wa-l-mashāhid al-mazūrah* (*Famed Tombs and Visited Shrines*); it has recently been edited. The work is referred to by Diem and Schöller in *The Living and the Dead in Islam*, 2:312, but they do not cite *Nisāʾ al-khulafāʾ*.

46 Jawād, "Introduction," 12.

47 Ibn al-Sāʿī's sources for the early- to mid-Abbasid consorts include Abū l-ʿAynāʾ, Abū Bakr al-Ṣūlī, Abū l-Faraj al-Iṣfahānī, ʿAlī ibn Yaḥyā the astromancer, Hilāl ibn al-Muḥassin the Sabian, Ibn al-Muʿtazz, Jaʿfar ibn Qudāmah, al-Jahshiyārī, Jaḥẓah, members of the al-Mawṣilī family, al-Ṭabarī, Thābit ibn Sinān, and Thaʿlab; for all of these, see the glossaries.

48 §3.3.

49 §6.4.

50 §13.1, §13.7.

51 §3.1: ʿInān; §6.5: ʿArīb; §6.7: an anonymous slave; §7.3: Bidʿah; §13.3; §13.5; §13.6; §13.9; §14.2: Faḍl; §15.3; §15.4; §15.5; §15.6: Maḥbūbah; §19.2; §19.3: Nabt.

52 §3.5; §3.7.

53 §6.5.

54 Ibn al-Sāʿī cites Abū l-Faraj al-Iṣfahānī as the author of the *Book of Songs*, but Abū l-Faraj al-Iṣfahānī also wrote a book devoted to women slave poets, *al-Imāʾ al-shawāʿir*, extant and available in two editions, both from 1983, one edited by al-Qaysī and al-Sāmarrāʾī (paginated), the other edited by al-ʿAṭiyyah (numbered). The texts of the two editions are not identical, but of our "consorts," both have: ʿInān (pages 23–44/no. 1); Faḍl (49–71/no. 3); Haylānah (95–96/no. 14); ʿArīb (99–112/no. 16); Maḥbūbah (117–20/no. 20); Banān/Bunān (121–22/no. 21); Nabt (129–31/no. 25); Bidʿah (139–141/no. 29). These references are given here because *al-Imāʾ al-shawāʿir* is not among the otherwise comprehensive list of sources cited in Jawād's footnotes

to *Jihāt al-a'immah*. (For a more recent edition of al-Iṣfahānī's book, titled *Riyy al-ẓamā fī-man qāla al-shi'r fī l-imā*, see Primary Sources in the bibliography.)

55 §13.4; §7.3; §7.4.

56 According to Ibn al-Sā'ī, Hārūn al-Rashīd married Ghādir (§2.1); we find the identical story in Ibn al-Jawzī, *al-Muntaẓam*, 8: 349, but al-Ṭabarī does not list her among Hārūn's wives (*The 'Abbāsid Caliphate in Equilibrium*, 326–27). Farīdah the Younger is said to have married al-Mutawakkil (§18.3); in the *Book of Songs*, in the joint entry on Farīdah the Elder and Farīdah the Younger, Abū l-Faraj al-Iṣfahānī (*Kitāb al-Aghānī*, 3:183), cites al-Ṣūlī as the authority for this; again, the "marriage" is not mentioned elsewhere. There is a question mark over these stories: the jurists would certainly have disapproved of a free man marrying a slave without first freeing her, but perhaps manumission is implied by the very word "marriage." Two other such women are said to have married free men: Farīdah the Elder marries twice, again with no mention of manumission (§11.1); and Sarīrah—who had borne her owner a child and thereby gained her freedom when he was killed—marries a Hamdanid prince (§36.1).

57 In addition to Jawād's footnotes to *Nisā' al-khulafā'*, see Stigelbauer, *Die Sängerinnen am Abbasidenhof um die Zeit des Kalifen al-Mutawakkil*; and Al-Heitty, *The Role of the Poetess at the Abbāsid Court (132–247 A.H./750–861 A.D.)*.

58 Kilpatrick, *Making the Great Book of Songs*.

59 Imhof, "Traditio vel Aemulatio? The Singing Contest of Sāmarrā."

60 Al-Jāḥiẓ (d. 255/868), *Risālat al-Qiyān/The Epistle on Singing-Girls*; al-Washshā' (d. 325/936), *Kitāb al-Muwashshā*, also known as *al-Ẓarf wa-l-ẓurafā'*, chapter 20. German and Spanish translations, as well as a partial French one, exist of *Kitāb al-Muwashshā*: *Das Buch des buntbestickten Kleids*, ed. Bellmann; *El libro del brocado*, ed. Garulo; *Le livre de brocart*, ed. Bouhlal.

61 Ali, *Marriage and Slavery in Early Islam*, is an important departure.

62 The other six members of RRAALL are Kristen Brustad, Jamal Elias, Nuha Khoury, Nasser Rabbat, Dwight Reynolds, and Eve Troutt Powell.

63 Reynolds, ed., *Interpreting the Self.*

64 And, helpfully, there appears to be only one extant manuscript of Ibn al-Sā ʿī's *Jihāt al-aʾimmah al-khulafāʾ min al-ḥarāʾir wa-l-imāʾ*, which is in the Veliyyuddin Library in Istanbul, bearing MS no. Veliyyuddin 2634. Muhammet Günaydın of Istanbul University kindly obtained a copy for us on CD from the Beyazıt Devlet Kütüphanesi (Beyazıt State Library) in 2012. The manuscript has 58 folios, the first 48 of which consist of *Jihāt al-aʾimmah.* Folios 49–58 comprise a miscellany of stories, some humorous, some moralistic, culled from the adab literary tradition. The colophon to *Jihāt al-aʾimmah* appears on the verso of folio 48. It states that the copying of the manuscript was completed on 4 Rajab, 900 [March 30, 1495] by one Muḥammad ibn Sālim al-Ḥāniʾ. It also mentions the fact that the book has been supplemented with "the consorts of princes and important viziers." This refers to the fact that in the latter part of the book, Ibn al-Sā ʿī includes entries about the consorts of a vizier and of several Saljūq sultans. There is one previous edition of the work, published as *Nisāʾ al-khulafāʾ*, first published by Dār al-Ma ʿārif in Cairo in 1962 as volume 28 in the "Dhakhā ʾir al- ʿArab" series and reprinted in 1968 and 1993. Manshūrāt al-Jamal issued a handsome reprint in 2011.

CONSORTS OF THE CALIPHS

In the name of God, Full of Compassion, Ever Compassionate,
in Whom I place my trust

By praising God, lord of all the worlds, I begin * and by pronouncing blessings upon our master Muḥammad and his kin. * Having compiled *The Lives of Those Gracious and Bounteous Consorts of Caliphs * Who Lived to See Their Own Sons Become Caliph* * I now wish to write * about famous favorites * whether consorts or concubines of caliphs. 0.1

God grant me success!

1

Ḥammādah bint ʿĪsā[1]

Wife of the Caliph al-Manṣūr

I cite the trustee ʿAbd al-Wahhāb ibn ʿAlī who gave me license to cite ʿAbd al-Raḥmān ibn Muḥammad al-Shaybānī, who cites master[2] Aḥmad ibn ʿAlī, who cites al-Ḥasan ibn Abī Bakr as saying that Abū Sahl Aḥmad ibn Muḥammad al-Qaṭṭān[3] said: 1.1

I heard Thaʿlab[4] say:

> When the caliph al-Manṣūr's wife, Ḥammādah daughter of ʿĪsā, died, al-Manṣūr and his retinue stood at the edge of the grave that had been dug for her and awaited the arrival of the funeral procession.
>
> The poet Abū Dulāmah was in the procession. Al-Manṣūr turned to him and asked, "What have you brought us on this sad occasion, Abū Dulāmah?"
>
> "The body of Ḥammādah daughter of ʿĪsā, Sire!" he replied, and everyone burst into laughter.[5]

2

Ghādir

"Inconstance"

SLAVE OF THE CALIPH AL-HĀDĪ

2.1 Jaʿfar ibn Qudāmah writes:[6]

Ghādir had the most beautiful face and voice and al-Hādī loved her intensely. As she was singing to him one day, a thought occurred to him. One of his close companions asked him why he was preoccupied.

"I've realized I'm going to die, and that my brother Hārūn will succeed me as caliph and marry my slave," he replied.

"God forbid!" everyone exclaimed, "May you outlive us all!"

Al-Hādī summoned his brother and told him about his misgivings, and Hārūn did his best to reassure him. But al-Hādī insisted, "Swear to me that when I die, you will not marry her!"

He had Hārūn swear that if he broke his vow, he would perform the hajj on foot, divorce all his wives, free all his slaves, and distribute everything he owned as alms. Al-Hādī also had Ghādir make a corresponding vow.

Less than a month later al-Hādī died. Hārūn was given the oath of allegiance, becoming the caliph al-Rashīd, and immediately sent an emissary to Ghādir, asking for her hand in marriage.

"What shall we do about the vow?" she asked.

"I'll pay an atonement for all the vows," al-Rashīd replied, "and perform the hajj on foot."

So she accepted his offer and he married her.

Al-Rashīd fell so deeply in love with Ghādir that he would place her head in his lap as she slept and would not move or shift position until she woke. 2.2

One day, she was asleep and woke up in a fright, sobbing.

Al-Rashīd asked what was troubling her, and she said, "I've just seen your brother in a dream and this is what he said:

When the dead became my neighbors
the vow you took meant nothing to you.
You forgot me and broke your word
your vow was a shameless lie.[7]
Treacherously you bedded my brother:
'Inconstance'—how well they named you!
I spend my nights with corpses,
you spend your days with dark-eyed beauties!
Curse your new love!
Disaster strike you!
Drop dead before morning!
As I am now, may you be too!

"I swear, Sire, I can almost hear him now! His words are graven on my heart and I can't get them out of my mind!"

«Muddled nightmares!»,[8] al-Rashīd replied, comforting her.

"No, no!" she cried, trembling. Then she gave a shudder and died on the spot.

This happened in the year 173 [789–90].

3

ʿInān, daughter of ʿAbd Allāh[9]

"Restraint"

Slave of al-Nāṭifī[10]

3.1 ʿInān was a poet and woman of wit about whom there is a written body of anecdotes.

3.2 Abū l-Faraj al-Iṣfahānī mentions her in the *Book of Songs*. He writes:

> Al-Nāṭifī's slave ʿInān was a blonde of mixed parentage, brought up and trained in al-Yamāmah.
>
> Al-Nāṭifī had purchased her and al-Rashīd wanted to buy her from him. But ʿInān's notoriety and the fact that many poets satirized her prevented him from doing so, although he was quite besotted and infatuated with her. The story goes that al-Rashīd sent for ʿInān and offered to buy her from al-Nāṭifī, who named a price of one hundred thousand silver dirhams. Al-Rashīd agreed, kept her for a while, but then sent her back. Relieved, her master al-Nāṭifī gave away thirty thousand dirhams in charity.
>
> When al-Nāṭifī died, she was sold for two hundred thousand dirhams.

3.3 ʿInān was the first poet to become famous under the Abbasids and the most gifted poet of her generation. The major male poets of the time would seek her out in her master's house where they would recite their verses to her and have her pass judgment.

When her master died, ʿInān was freed—either because he had bequeathed her her freedom in his will or because she had borne him a child.[11] 3.4

Citing sources going back to Marwān ibn Abī Ḥafṣah, Abū l-Faraj al-Iṣfahānī reports that Marwān said: 3.5

> One day I ran into al-Nāṭifī, who invited me to come and meet ʿInān. We went to his house and he entered her room ahead of me saying, "Look, I've brought you the greatest poet of all—Marwān ibn Abī Ḥafṣah!"
>
> ʿInān was not feeling well and said, "I have other things than Marwān to worry about right now!"
>
> Al-Nāṭifī struck her with his whip and called out to me, "Come on in!"
>
> I entered and found her weeping. Seeing her tears, I extemporized:
>
> *ʿInān weeps tears that scatter*
> *like a broken string of pearls.*
>
> She immediately responded with:
>
> *May the tyrant's right arm wither*
> *as his cruel whip unfurls!*
>
> "If any man or jinn[12] alive is a greater poet than she, I'll free every single slave I own!" I said to al-Nāṭifī.

Abū l-Faraj al-Iṣfahānī reports that al-Jawharī cites ʿUmar ibn Shabbah, who cites Aḥmad ibn Muʿāwiyah, who said: 3.6

> I heard someone say:
>
> While leafing through some books, I came across a verse that I was hoping someone could cap, but however hard I tried, I couldn't find anyone. A friend said to me,

"You should go see ʿInān, al-Nāṭifī's slave." So I did, and I recited the verse to her:

He complained of love so long
that his whole body sighed and spoke!

Without a moment's hesitation she rejoined with:

He weeps, and pitying him I weep—
he weeps tears, but on tears of blood I choke.

3.7 Abū l-Faraj al-Iṣfahānī reports—citing Aḥmad ibn ʿUbayd Allāh, who cites ʿAbd Allāh ibn Abī Saʿd, citing Masʿūd ibn ʿĪsā—that Mūsā ibn ʿAbd Allāh al-Tamīmī recounted the following:

Abū Nuwās went to see al-Nāṭifī and found his slave ʿInān weeping because her master had struck her. Her cheek was pressed against the door latch. Al-Nāṭifī made a sign to Abū Nuwās to compose a verse to get her to move and Abū Nuwās declaimed:

ʿInān, won't you treat an old man with kindness?
I'm at «The Emissary believes and sets store . . . .»

—meaning he was at the "end" of his life, since the line «The Emissary believes and sets store in that which his Lord revealed to him . . . .» comes at the end of Surah Baqarah in the Qur'an.[13]

ʿInān came back with:

If you persist in severing all bonds with me—
please don't—then I'm "done" for.[14]

Abū Nuwās rejoined:

Ruthless, the one I love would destroy
the quick and the dead with no regret.

And ʿInān came back with:

On granite trained, his languid eye
would sickness in the stone beget.

Abū l-Faraj al-Iṣfahānī reports, citing Jaʿfar ibn Qudāmah, who cites Abū l-ʿAynāʾ, that al-ʿAbbās ibn Rustam said: 3.8

Abān al-Lāḥiqī and I went to see al-Nāṭifī's slave ʿInān one summer's day. She was sitting in a room cooled by dampened canvas sheets and a fan, and Abān said to her:

Summer's pleasure is a room well fanned!

She replied:

Not opposing armies making a stand![15]

Then I said:

Every day new chamomiles
make the earth laugh from heaven's tears.

And she came back with:

Like brocade on Sanaa silk
that traders bring from Yemen's frontiers.[16]

*

Then Abān goaded her, saying, "Jarīr's verse is certainly beautiful, the one which goes:

I show a brave face to my companions
though your love has me on the hook."[17]

And without hesitation she came back with:

When tongues are hocked by fear,
then eyes reveal all with a look.[18]

Jaʿfar ibn Qudāmah and Jaḥẓah both report: 3.9

Hibat Allāh the son of Ibrāhīm ibn al-Mahdī recited the following verses, which his father had heard declaimed by al-Nāṭifī's slave ʿInān:

My soul is given over to sighing,
if only it would depart with those sighs!
If my fate were in my hands
I would race to my demise.
No good remains now that you're gone:
an outstretched life, I fear, before me lies!

Abū l-Faraj al-Iṣfahānī writes, "With these verses, ʿInān lamented her master al-Nāṭifī."

3.10 Abū l-ʿAynāʾ quoted al-Jammāz and others as saying that Abū Nuwās challenged al-Nāṭifī's slave ʿInān to respond to a verse, and she responded as follows . . .[19] *

3.11 Abū l-Faraj al-Iṣfahānī records that ʿInān journeyed to Egypt and died there in the year 226 [840–41].

4

Ghaḍīḍ

"Luscious"

Slave of the Caliph al-Rashīd and Mother of His Daughter Ḥamdūnah

Abū Jaʿfar Muḥammad ibn Jarīr al-Ṭabarī writes in his *History* that 4.1
her name was Muṣaffā, "Pure."[20] She was an authority on the poetry of Maẓlūmah, "Ill-Treated," the slave of ʿAbbāsah, daughter of the caliph al-Mahdī.

Ghaḍīḍ was a favored concubine of al-Rashīd's and part of his inner circle. She died during his caliphate.

5

Haylānah

"Voilà"[21]

Slave of the Caliph al-Rashīd

5.1 Al-Rashīd got her from Yaḥyā ibn Khālid the Barmakid. She was extraordinarily lovely and accomplished. She enjoyed al-Rashīd's favor until her death three years later. In his great sorrow he wrote the following elegy:

When they laid you in earth
my breast was racked with grief.
I said to myself, "Die—
there's no more joy in life!"

Al-ʿAbbās ibn al-Aḥnaf composed a forty-line elegy on Haylānah, for which al-Rashīd gave him forty thousand dirhams—a thousand for each line.[22]

She died in the year 173 [789–90].

6

ʿArīb al-Maʾmūniyyah

"Ardent"

Member of the Household of the Caliph al-Maʾmūn

She was said to be the daughter of Jaʿfar ibn Yaḥyā ibn Khālid the Barmakid. She was stolen and sold as a child when the Barmakids fell from power. She was bought by al-Rashīd's son al-Amīn, who then sold her to his brother al-Maʾmūn. She excelled as a poet and also as a singer and musician. 6.1

I was informed by the trustee ʿAbd al-Wahhāb ibn ʿAlī[23]—who cites Ibn Nāṣir, citing al-Mubārak ibn ʿAbd al-Jabbār al-Ṣayrafī, citing Ibrāhīm ibn ʿUmar al-Barmakī, who heard it from ʿUbayd Allāh ibn Muḥammad al-ʿUkbarī, who heard it from Abū Bakr Muḥammad ibn al-Qāsim al-Anbārī, who heard it from his father, Abū Muḥammad al-Anbārī,[24] who heard it from Abū Hāshim, who heard it from Maymūn ibn Hārūn the state secretary—that ʿArīb used to tell the following story: 6.2

> Hārūn al-Rashīd sent a messenger to my people—she meant the Barmakids, whom al-Rashīd had overthrown; she maintained that she was the daughter of Jaʿfar ibn

Yaḥyā—to ask after them, having instructed him not to reveal who had sent him.

The messenger went to my uncle, al-Faḍl ibn Yaḥyā, and asked, "What news? What cheer?"

My uncle replied as follows:

"How are you?" they ask. Our answer is this—
"How do you think, when our star has set?
Our clan, victims of Fate's caprice,
are evermore by misfortune beset."

6.3 Abū Bakr al-Ṣūlī writes:[25]

> ʿArīb al-Maʾmūniyyah claimed to be the daughter of Jaʿfar son of Yaḥyā son of Khālid the Barmakid by a lady of noble birth. She was a poet and also set many poems to music; her collected songs form a discrete work.
>
> The following is an example of one of her own poems that she set to music:
>
> *Enough! I won't be duped again.*
> *you've made me every kind of fool!*
> *You change so often—what's to be done?*
> *your heart isn't mine to rule.*

6.4 I was informed by ʿAbd al-Raḥmān ibn Saʿd Allāh al-Daqīqī, who cites Abū l-Qāsim ibn al-Samarqandī, citing Abū Manṣūr al-ʿUkbarī, citing Abū l-Ḥasan ibn al-Ṣalt, citing Abū l-Faraj al-Iṣfahānī, who said: I heard from Muḥammad ibn Mazyad and Yaḥyā ibn ʿAlī, both citing Ḥammād ibn Isḥāq, who said that his father Isḥāq al-Mawṣilī told him the following:

> I never saw a more beautiful or refined woman than ʿArīb, nor one who sang, played music, wrote poetry, or played chess so well. She possessed every quality of elegance and skill one could wish for in a woman.

6.5 The same source also quotes Abū l-Faraj al-Iṣfahānī, who heard from Jaḥẓah that ʿAlī ibn Yaḥyā the astromancer told him:

One day, I left the caliph al-Muʿtamid's court and headed for ʿArīb's place. Before I reached her house, I got caught in the rain and my clothes were soaked through.

When I arrived, my clothes were taken and I was given a ceremonial robe to wear. Food was brought and we sat and ate. Then ʿArīb called for wine, dismissed her women, and asked me how the caliph had been earlier that day, what music he had listened to, and who had performed it.

I told her that Bunān[26] had sung the following to the caliph:

He weeps and grieves
as the tribe leaves.[27]
Anxious, uneasy,
he was once carefree!
Love has put him in danger—
of burning up.
And his lids are sleepless,
wide open or shut!

When she heard this, she sent one of her people to fetch Bunān, who came at once. After he had had some food and wine, he was given a lute and ʿArīb asked him to improvise a song to the following verses of hers:

The rain has showered
and the jonquil has flowered.
Fill a cup to the brink
with bubbles that wink,
Whose splendorous glim
almost burns the rim.
Now Bunān has sung to us:
"And his lids are sleepless"![28]

Bunān applied the melody from the earlier song to these verses and sang them to us for the rest of the day.

6.6 The same source quotes Jaʿfar ibn Qudāmah as saying that Ibn al-Muʿtazz told him:

> Some of ʿArīb's correspondence came into my possession, notes in both prose and verse. The following is a letter she wrote to al-Maʾmūn when he had gone to Fam al-Ṣilḥ to marry Būrān:
>
> *Live happily ever after*
> *with Būrān!*
> *A cherished pearl whose star*
> *follows the lofty course of Maʾmūn!*
> *In a lap that's surely blessed—*
> *Būrān's!—kingship has come to rest.*

6.7 According to the secretary ʿAlī ibn Shādhān, ʿArīb al-Maʾmūniyyah related:

> I once accompanied the caliph al-Wāthiq as he made the rounds of his slaves before setting off on an outing to al-Anbār. He called on Farīdah, a slave he loved very much.[29] He was also infatuated with one of Farīdah's servants, and I was the only one who knew about it. When this servant saw al-Wāthiq with her mistress, she went to her dressing-room to fetch something. She came back and stood beside Farīdah, wearing a ribbon around her head on which the following words were written in gold:
>
> *I fear to part—*
> *my hot eyes smart.*
> *Love hurts most*
> *when sweethearts part!*
>
> "ʿArīb, do you follow?" al-Wāthiq asked me.
>
> "I do, my lord," I replied.
>
> Using a stick he was carrying, he wrote out on the ground the following lines, which I committed to memory:

In full view, passion has rent its veil:
love's best course is to be in plain sight.
Who cares for carpers? Speak your desire!
Lovers professed know the greatest delight.

We laughed and Farīdah caught on. She said, "Sire, I see how it is with the two of you. Do your servant the kindness of accepting her."

"With pleasure!" said al-Wāthiq. "ʿArīb, take charge of her."

As I led her away, he was unable to keep himself in check and ran after me in his haste to be alone with her. And he ordered that I be given a thousand gold dinars!

ʿUbayd Allāh son of Ibn Abī Ṭāhir writes that al-Maʾmūn's slave[30] 6.8
ʿArīb died in the month of Rabiʿ al-Thani, 277 [July–August, 890]. According to other sources, she died in Samarra at the age of ninety-six, which would mean she was born in the year 181 [797].[31]

7

Bidʿah al-Kabīrah

"Nova" the Elder

SLAVE OF ʿARĪB
AND DEPENDENT IN THE HOUSEHOLD
OF THE CALIPH AL-MAʾMŪN

7.1 Abū l-Faraj al-Iṣfahānī reports that she was the most beautiful and best singer of her time and that she was well regarded for the light verse she composed.

7.2 Thābit ibn Sinān the Sabian physician mentions in his *History* that Isḥāq ibn Ayyūb al-Ghālibī paid Bidʿah's mistress ʿArīb one hundred thousand dinars for her,[32] through the intermediary of ʿAlī ibn Yaḥyā the astromancer, to whom he promised a further twenty thousand dinars for his mediation.

When ʿAlī ibn Yaḥyā brought the matter up with ʿArīb, she summoned Bidʿah, introduced them, and asked her, "Do you consent, and do you choose to be sold?"

Bidʿah let her know that she did not, so ʿArīb returned the money and freed her on the spot.

7.3 Abū l-Faraj al-Iṣfahānī reports that Bidʿah's handler ʿArafah related as follows:

When the caliph al-Muʿtaḍid returned from Syria with Waṣīf the Eunuch as his prisoner, Bidʿah went to see him the first day he held court.[33]

"Bidʿah!" he said, "Can't you see how my beard and hair 'blaze white'?"[34] "My lord," she replied, "May God give you eternal life, and let you see your own grandsons' hair turn white! By God, your silvery hair is more beautiful than the moon." She paused a while, then declaimed * the following lines:

White hair has done you no harm
your beauty has only increased.
Time has polished you
and you are without flaw.
Flourish and be happy,
set your mind at rest.
With every day that passes,
your good fortune grows
In blessings and contentment—
your star is ascendant.

Al-Muʿtaḍid rewarded her with a magnificent gift and sent her home with many fine clothes and perfumes.

Abū l-Faraj al-Iṣfahānī also reports from ʿArafah as follows: 7.4

When al-Muʿtaḍid brought Waṣīf captive from the battlefield, he received Bidʿah, who said, "God, how this expedition has aged you, Sire!"

"Lesser things have turned a man's hair white," he replied.

As she was leaving, she sang the following poem she had composed:

Ruler of all the world, though you've aged and matured
through all the hardships you've endured
White hair makes you fairer—
wisdom's sign, perfected in the bearer.

May you live twice as long again
in ease and plenty, in might and main!

Al-Muʿtaḍid was touched and rewarded her with a purse and ceremonial robes.

7.5 Muḥammad ibn ʿImrān al-Marzubānī reports that al-Muẓaffar ibn Yaḥyā al-Sharābī cited ʿArafah, the manager of Bidʿah's affairs, who related that one day he went to see Bidʿah and found her eating a dish of Eggplant à la Būrān.[35] Her eyes were inflamed so he asked, "Why do you eat it if it makes you cry?" "Do you leave someone you love just because he hurts you?" she replied.

7.6 Thābit ibn Sinān[36] records the following in his *History*:

> ʿArīb's slave, Bidʿah the Elder, passed away on the twenty-fourth of Dhu l-Hijjah in the year 302 [July 10, 915]. Abū Bakr the son of the caliph al-Muhtadī led the funeral prayers.[37]

8

Būrān

Daughter of al-Ḥasan ibn Sahl, al-Ma'mūn's Vizier[38]

As Abū Bakr al-Ṣūlī notes, her given name was Khadījah but she was known as Būrān. 8.1

Al-Ṭabarī reports that al-Ma'mūn was married to her in the year 202 [817] and did not consummate the marriage until the month of Ramadan, 210 [December 825–January 826], in the town of Fam al-Ṣilḥ.[39] 8.2

On their first night, Būrān's grandmother ceremonially bestrewed her with over a thousand large pearls from a golden tray. Al-Ma'mūn then ordered that the pearls be gathered up. They were collected and returned to the platter. Al-Ma'mūn set the platter in Būrān's lap and said, "This is your wedding present. Tell me what else you desire."

Būrān's grandmother said, "Do as your lord says. Tell him what you want, as he instructs!"

So Būrān asked him to pardon his uncle Ibrāhīm ibn al-Mahdī.[40]

"Done," said al-Ma'mūn.

Then she asked him to grant his stepmother Zubaydah permission to perform the hajj, to which he also agreed.[41] For this Zubaydah rewarded Būrān with the Umayyads' jewel-studded surcoat.[42]

Al-Ma'mūn consummated the marriage that same night. For the occasion, a candle of ambergris weighing seventy pounds was lit and set in a candelabrum made of gold.[43]

8.3.1 Al-Ma'mūn remained with his father-in-law al-Ḥasan ibn Sahl for seventeen days. Al-Ḥasan provided al-Ma'mūn and his entourage with all their needs every single day and also distributed ceremonial robes, horses, and cash to the caliph's commanders, each according to his rank. The total outlay was fifty million dirhams.

When al-Ma'mūn left, he ordered that ten thousand dinars from the tax revenues of Fārs be sent to al-Ḥasan. Al-Ma'mūn also granted him the revenues from the district of al-Ṣilḥ. These revenues, which had already been tallied, were brought directly to al-Ḥasan, who summoned his commanders, close officials, retainers, and servants and distributed the money among them.

8.3.2 Al-Ḥasan ibn Sahl's son Aḥmad reported the following:

> Our family used to talk about how my father wrote out the names of estates on slips of paper and strewed them among his commanders and among the members of the Hāshimī clan. Whoever got a slip with the name of a particular estate on it sent a messenger to take possession of that estate.

8.3.3 Al-Jahshiyārī writes that 'Abd al-Wāḥid ibn Muḥammad cited the dependent of al-Ḥasan, 'Alī ibn Sahl ibn Abān, who said:[44]

> The day of the marriage-contract celebration, al-Ḥasan scattered pellets of ambergris,[45] a gesture that everyone at first found uncouth. Then al-Ḥasan ordered that the tossed pellets be cracked open. He assigned a man to each recipient to make sure his intentions would be carried out. When the pellets were split open some had slips of paper

in them, each of which entitled the recipient to a piece of land or other allocation.

Ibrāhīm ibn al-ʿAbbās subsequently addressed the following poem to al-Ḥasan: 8.3.4

You are blessed with such in-laws! The proud are abased
and the arrogant are humbled, through the glory of this troth.
The Hāshimīs are reunited with Kisrā's line:[46]
Kisrā's progeny are honored by your oath.
Your sons are now the Prophet's kin, and caliphs' heirs,
and successors of Kisrā and Hāshim both!

Abū Bakr al-Ṣūlī cites ʿAwn ibn Muḥammad, who says that ʿAbd 8.4
Allāh ibn Abī Sahl told him the following:

When al-Ma'mūn consummated his marriage to al-Ḥasan ibn Sahl's daughter Būrān, he journeyed to his in-laws, sailing down the Tigris toward Wāsiṭ.

On the day of the consummation, a gold-woven mat was spread for him, and many precious pearls were scattered on it. The whiteness of the pearls glittered against the gold of the mat, and no one wanted to touch them. Al-Ḥasan sent a message to al-Ma'mūn, saying, "These gems are a bestowal. Let the guests help themselves to them."

So al-Ma'mūn turned to the princesses who were present and commanded, "Honor al-Ḥasan's gift!" Each princess reached out and took one pearl, leaving the rest to glitter on the gold-woven mat.

All of a sudden, al-Ma'mūn exclaimed, "Damn that Abū Nuwās! He was able to describe scenes without ever having witnessed them! How brilliantly he described the froth on wine when he said:

Bubbles like pearls on a floor of gold.

Just imagine what he would have said if he'd he seen the thing for himself!"

Abū Nuwās had by that time already passed away.

8.5 Abū ʿAlī al-Kawkabī reports that Abū l-Faḍl al-Rabaʿī told him that his father said:

> Just as al-Ma'mūn was about to take Būrān's virginity on their wedding night, her period started. She quoted the Qur'anic verse, «God's command is nigh; do not be hasty»[47] and al-Ma'mūn, realizing what she meant, leapt off her.

8.6 Al-Jahshiyārī writes that Ibn Ḥamdūn mentions the following poem composed by Būrān to mourn al-Ma'mūn:

Weep, my eyes! The Caliph has passed on
and I'm a captive to melancholy.
Once I was the one who ravaged fate;
now he's gone, fate ravages me.

8.7 The state secretary Hilāl ibn al-Muḥassin reports that Būrān was born on Monday night the third of Safar in the year 192 [December 6, 807]. But ʿUbayd Allāh son of Ibn Abī Ṭāhir reports that Būrān died at the age of eighty on Tuesday the twenty-seventh of Rabiʿ al-Awwal in the year 271 [September 21, 884].[48]

8.8.1 Būrān must have died in Baghdad, since she lived in the Ḥasanī palace, named after her father al-Ḥasan ibn Sahl. This palace was originally called the Jaʿfarī palace, after Jaʿfar the Barmakid; it was the first building built in the early days of East Baghdad.[49]

8.8.2 Abū l-Qāsim ʿAlī ibn ʿAbd al-Raḥmān informed me—citing Abū Muḥammad ʿAbd Allāh ibn al-Khashshāb[50] the grammarian, with his permission, who cites Abū l-Qāsim al-Rabaʿī, citing the supreme judge Abū l-Ḥasan al-Māwardī, who cites Abū ʿAlī al-Azdī, who cites al-Jammāz[51]—that Abū l-ʿAynā' related the following:

> Jaʿfar ibn Yaḥyā the Barmakid was very attached to his friends and enamored of his singing-girls. He gave free rein

to his pleasures and regularly scheduled days of revelry and dalliance. This became so excessive that he became notorious and tongues began to wag.

His father took him aside and reprimanded him in private for his conduct. “If you can’t enjoy your revelry and drink discreetly and keep your antics hidden,” he said, “then build yourself a palace on the East Bank where you can get together with your drinking companions and singing-girls. Over there, out of the public eye, your time can be your own and your affairs can remain largely hidden from the court. This will stop people talking, put an end to the rumors, and raise your standing with your sovereign.”

So Jaʿfar built a palace of vast proportions on the East Bank, with a large open court and a garden full of fruit trees of every kind. He poured great sums of money into it and employed an army of laborers and craftsmen to work on it.

When it was almost finished, he took his friends out to see it, among them the shrewd and clever Muʾnis ibn ʿImrān. Jaʿfar walked around the palace and found it to be superb. All his companions raved about how wonderful it was, except for Muʾnis, who was silent.

“What’s wrong?” Jaʿfar asked him, “Why aren’t you saying anything?”

“About what?” replied Muʾnis.

“About what everyone else is talking about!”

“They’ve said it all; I’ve nothing to add,” said Muʾnis.

Jaʿfar was astute enough to realize that there was something behind Muʾnis’s words, and asked him pointedly, “But what do you have to say?”

“No, really,” replied Muʾnis, “it’s as they’ve said.”

“I demand that you speak!” Jaʿfar ordered.

“Since you insist I say something,” said Muʾnis, “can you handle the truth?”

“Of course I can,” replied Jaʿfar.

“It needs to be in private.”

When they were alone, Mu'nis asked, "Do you want the long version or the short?"

"Give me the short version," Jaʿfar said.

"Imagine going out right now and finding that one of your own entourage had built a palace more or less like this one. What do you think you'd say? And how do you think you'd react?"

"Point taken," said Jaʿfar. "What should I do?"

"What I'm going to suggest, you must do immediately or else it'll be too late."

"Which is?" asked Jaʿfar.

"I have no doubt that the caliph has been asking for you and been told that you've gone out to your palace. He's probably annoyed with you for staying away so long. Stay a while longer, then rush to his palace and appear before him with your clothes still dusty. When he asks what you've been up to, say, 'I've been out at the palace I'm building for al-Ma'mūn,' then use your own discretion."

8.8.3 Here our source, Abū l-ʿAynāʾ, notes that Jaʿfar's palace had three hundred and sixty rooms, including formal sitting rooms, balconies, bedrooms, rooms furnished with dampened canvas sheets to cool the air, and storerooms. Jaʿfar had sent away for sets of rugs and cushions to be procured from every corner of the empire, all custom-made to fit each separate chamber. There was no end of talk and speculation about the building and the furnishings that had been ordered for it.

8.8.4 Cutting short his stay, Jaʿfar hurried off to see al-Rashīd, who asked him where he had been and what he had been doing.

"I've been at the palace I've built on the East Bank for my master, al-Ma'mūn," he replied.

"Oh, you built it for al-Ma'mūn, did you?" Hārūn asked.

"Absolutely, Sire," he replied, "because on the night he was born, you honored me by placing him in my lap before placing him in your own, and honored me by making me his servant. Knowing full well how dear he is to you, I was inspired to build a palace for him on the East Bank, where the climate is moderate and the soil very good. It has flowering gardens and flowing streams and is far from noisy crowds, noxious vapors, and nasty smells. His nursemaids, wet nurses, housemaids and housekeepers can all live with him. There, his humors will be balanced and he will grow up healthy, clear-minded, pure-hearted, and intelligent, and he will develop superior understanding, a good complexion, and strong limbs. What's more, I've sent away to all the provinces for custom-made furnishings, though there are still a few items I haven't been able to obtain. I'm hoping I can rely on the caliphal treasury for a loan, or a gift. . . ."

"A gift, of course!" said al-Rashīd. He then parted the curtain and faced Jaʿfar directly. "God forbid that anyone falsely accuse or slander you! May people only praise and honor you! You alone shall occupy that palace, by God! And we alone shall provide the remaining furnishings."

Al-Rashīd's suspicions were allayed by this ploy. Jaʿfar got to keep the palace and rumors about him ceased. He went there whenever he wanted to revel or relax, and continued to do so until the caliph al-Rashīd deposed the Barmakids and they fell from grace. Until that time, it was known as the Jaʿfarī Palace.

How the Palace Became the Property of al-Maʾmūn; and the Additions He Made to It

According to one source, the palace subsequently became the property of al-Maʾmūn. Truly a splendid palace, it was the one he most cherished—because it overlooked the Tigris, was beautiful to behold, was enfolded by gardens and trees, and was adorned with brilliant and dazzling flowers. It was the palace in which he most preferred to spend his time. He would go there often to unwind, to stroll through its gardens, and to race his horses; he would thoroughly enjoy his stay and be rejuvenated by its fresh air. It soon 8.9

became his main retreat for the hunt and the chase, and for picnics and outings.

In addition, he enclosed a large neighboring tract of land and built a racecourse for his personal guard, a polo-ground, and a game preserve where he could hunt. He built an entrance on its eastern side facing the open country. Above it he built a platform that looked out over a vast expanse allowing a view of anyone arriving on the Khurasan Road and from the direction of Hamadhan or Azerbaijan.

He also diverted a watercourse from the Muʿallā Canal toward that entrance and had residences built along it and near it, assigning them to his retinue, courtiers and women. The area was known as al-Ma'mūniyyah. It is now the quarter through which passes the main thoroughfare between the Artificer's Archway and the Armorers' Archway.

How the Palace Became the Property of al-Ḥasan ibn Sahl; How It Was Named after Him; and the Additions He Made to It

8.10 When his father al-Rashīd died in Khurasan, al-Ma'mūn was with him and was given the oath of allegiance there; his brother al-Amīn was given the oath of allegiance in Baghdad. The great Civil War ensued, which lasted until al-Amīn was killed—may God have mercy on him. When the courier arrived and gave al-Ma'mūn the news that his brother had been killed, he sent al-Ḥasan ibn Sahl to be his deputy in Iraq. Al-Ḥasan reached Baghdad in the year 198 [813–14], at the end of the Civil War, and took up residence in the Ma'mūnī Palace.

Al-Ma'mūn married al-Ḥasan's daughter Būrān, with her uncle al-Faḍl ibn Sahl serving as her legal guardian for the betrothal. When al-Ma'mūn arrived from Khurasan on Saturday the sixteenth of Safar in the year 204 [August 12, 819], he took up residence in the Khuld[52] Caliphal Palace on the West Side of Baghdad. Al-Ḥasan remained at the Ma'mūnī Palace until Būrān's wedding was concluded in

Fam al-Ṣilḥ. When she was brought to Baghdad and lodged there, al-Ḥasan asked al-Maʾmūn for the palace and al-Maʾmūn gave it to him. It was then that al-Ḥasan made additions to it and that it came to be associated with him and his name.

Ibn Abī Ṭāhir says in his *Book of Baghdad* that one of his teachers told him:[53] 8.11

> When al-Ḥasan ibn Sahl renovated this palace, he left a large area unbuilt between its walls and the riverbank. Someone said, "You should have extended the palace walls all the way to the Tigris"; but he said, "When would I be able to stroll and gaze at the Tigris? That's only for people with time on their hands. We are far too busy."

Later, al-Muwaffaq bought the palace and took up residence there. 8.12
The caliph al-Muʿtaḍid subsequently razed it, rebuilt it, made additions, and extended it up to the embankment of the Bīn Canal.[54] Al-Muktafī then lived there.

9

Mu'nisah al-Ma'mūniyyah

"Chérie"

A Byzantine Slave, Member of the Household of the Caliph al-Ma'mūn

9.1 She was one of al-Ma'mūn's concubines and part of his inner circle. She took al-Ma'mūn's vizier, Aḥmad ibn Yūsuf, under her wing. He in turn served her and looked after her interests.

On one occasion, she went too far with al-Ma'mūn. He rebuffed her, leaving her behind when he traveled to his residence in al-Shammāsiyyah.[55] So she summoned Aḥmad's eunuch, Nuṣrah, and gave him a letter for his master, describing her plight and asking him to devise a way to patch things up between al-Ma'mūn and her.

When Aḥmad learned what had happened, he rode to al-Shammāsiyyah and requested an audience with al-Ma'mūn, saying, "I come as a messenger."

Aḥmad describes what happened next:

> Al-Ma'mūn gave me permission to deliver the message and I recited these verses to him:
>
> *Your censure before was a secret,*
> *today it's public, no longer hidden.*

Our enemies have won—may they not rejoice—
seeing you depart, leaving me forsaken.
I erred, but it is your custom, even when wronged,
to be lenient—may I be forgiven.

"Understood!" al-Ma'mūn said, "Now you can be a messenger of forgiveness," and he sent Yāsir the Eunuch to bring Mu'nisah to him.

10

Qurrat al-ʿAyn

"Solace"

DEPENDENT IN THE HOUSEHOLD OF THE CALIPH AL-MUʿTAṢIM

10.1 She was a slave of mixed parentage and a favorite of the caliph al-Muʿtaṣim—God be pleased with him. Judge Aḥmad ibn Kāmil transmitted literary material from her. She was very cultured and refined.

10.2 Abū Muḥammad al-Junābidhī informed us—citing Abū Bakr al-Ḥanbalī, who cites Abū Ghālib al-Karkhī, citing ʿUbayd Allāh ibn Aḥmad al-Azharī, who cites Ibrāhīm ibn Makhlad—that Judge Aḥmad ibn Kāmil said:

> Qurrat al-ʿAyn, the slave of al-Muʿtaṣim, recited the following verses to us:
>
> *Look on me with an eye of pardon for my lapses;*
> *don't leave me in fear and uncertainty.*
> *Your soul and mine are yoked together.*
> *How can we be apart without it killing me?*

11

Farīdah

"Solitaire"

Member of the Household of the Caliph al-Amīn

According to Abū Bakr al-Ṣūlī, her name is correctly spelled "Farīdah" with a long "i."[56] Two slave singers went by that name, one older, one younger. This Farīdah was the older one. 11.1

She was a slave of mixed parentage who grew up in the Hijaz. She came into the possession of Harūn al-Rashīd's chamberlain, al-Rabīʿ ibn Yūnus,[57] and learned to sing in his household.

She then became the property of the Barmakid family. When Jaʿfar ibn Yaḥyā was killed and the Barmakids were disgraced, Farīdah went into hiding. The caliph al-Rashīd searched for her without success. After al-Rashīd died, she became al-Amīn's. She remained with him until he was killed in the month of Muharram, 198 [September, 813], when she fled.

She later married al-Haytham ibn Bassām and bore him a son, ʿAbd Allāh. When al-Haytham died, she married al-Sindī ibn al-Ḥarashī, in whose household she died.

12

Isḥāq al-Andalusiyyah[58]

"Isaac" the Andalusian

12.1 She was a slave of mixed parentage and belonged to the caliph al-Mutawakkil. She was one of his favorites and the mother of his sons Ibrāhīm al-Mu'ayyad and Abū Aḥmad al-Muwaffaq.

12.2 ʿUbayd Allāh son of Ibn Abī Ṭāhir writes:

> Isḥāq, the mother of al-Muwaffaq, died in Baghdad on the eighteenth of Jumada al-Thani in the year 270 [December 23, 883]. She was buried in al-Ruṣāfah.

12.3 ʿAlī ibn Yaḥyā the astromancer composed the following poem to console al-Muwaffaq on the death of his mother Isḥāq:

Take heart—fate gives, and fate takes away;
be strong—nothing in this world remains constant.
For each one who gives in to grief, another withstands it:
there is no escaping God's commandment.
The heart cannot bear the sting of separation
nor can the eye hold back its tears.
The arrow of death must hit its mark
but noblest is he who stands firm.

Though the world teaches that nothing is forever
we play on, and pay no heed.
It destroys one abode after another,
and raises a new one, which falls as decreed.
Your loss is great—let your strength be greater!
Strength mends what grief has undone.
All of mankind is victim to disaster:
disaster past, disaster yet to come.
May her palace in Ruṣāfah stand forever,
watered by every passing cloud,
Singled out, as it deserves, for God's blessings,
which pours down on it, day and night.
A shelter for piety, virtue and devotion,
all graced by self-command.
As at the time of the setting sun:
Baghdad turned dark when she was gone.
She has passed; now praise follows her bier.
Those who mourn her speak true—
She is not dead! She leaves behind the Prince
and those who trace to her their line or due.
To die before you, when you fulfilled her hopes
was all she asked of her Lord.
Both prayers He granted:
her life-giving bounty still pours forth.
Take heart: her sacrifice safeguards you.
Live on! Feared by enemies, beloved by your folk.
Accept this respite: the arrows of misfortune,
so hard to bear, too easily find their mark.

13

Faḍl al-Shāʿirah al-Yamāmiyyah[59]

"Boon" the Poetess from al-Yamāmah

SLAVE OF THE CALIPH AL-MUTAWAKKIL—GOD SHOW HIM MERCY

13.1 She was a poet who composed racy verse and was one of the greatest wits of her time. Many amusing anecdotes about her are preserved in books.

13.2.1 According to what was reported to me by ʿAbd al-Raḥmān ibn Saʿd Allāh al-Daqīqī—who cites Abū l-Qāsim ibn al-Samarqandī, who cites Abū Manṣūr al-ʿUkbarī, who cites Abū l-Ḥasan ibn al-Ṣalt—Abū l-Faraj al-Iṣfahānī described her as follows:

> Faḍl was a slave of mixed parentage from Basra, where she was raised. She was born in al-Yamāmah.

13.2.2 She is also mentioned by Muḥammad ibn Dāwūd ibn al-Jarrāḥ, who writes that she was of the ʿAbd al-Qays tribe, a descent she also claimed for herself.[60] As she told it, her mother had been the dependent of an ʿAbd al-Qays tribesman who got her pregnant and who died while she was expecting her. The tribesman's son then sold her mother off and Faḍl was born into slavery.

According to another source, her mother gave birth to her while her father was still alive. He brought her up and educated her, but when he died his sons colluded to sell her. She was purchased by Muḥammad ibn al-Faraj al-Rukhkhajī, the brother of ʿUmar ibn al-Faraj,[61] who gave her to the caliph al-Mutawakkil.

She was dark-skinned, cultured, eloquent, and could think on her feet. Poetry came naturally to her, and she was better at it than all the other women of her time. 13.2.3

Via the authorities listed above,[62] Abū l-Faraj al-Iṣfahānī cites Muḥammad ibn Khalaf, who cites Ibn Abī Ṭāhir, who told him: 13.3

> Faḍl the Poetess was brought from Basra, and a slave trader bought her for ten thousand dirhams. Muḥammad ibn al-Faraj al-Rukhkhajī then bought her and gave her to al-Mutawakkil. She would sit on a dais at his gatherings in full view and improvise responses to the verses declaimed by other poets.
>
> One day, Abū Dulaf al-Qāsim ibn ʿĪsā al-ʿIjlī challenged her with:
>
> *They said, "You love a girl too young."*
> *I said, "The best mount is unridden, unyoked;*
> *What a difference between a pearl that's drilled and strung*
> *and one that's still unpoked!"*
>
> Faḍl came back with:
>
> *Riding is no pleasure till*
> *the mount's been broken to your will.*
> *And pearls are useless to their owners*
> *until they're drilled and strung.*

Via the same line of transmitters Abū l-Faraj al-Iṣfahānī relates that he heard Muḥammad ibn Khalaf, Jaʿfar ibn Qudāmah, and his own uncle[63] say that they heard Abū l-ʿAynāʾ report the following: 13.4

When Faḍl the Poetess was brought before al-Mutawakkil the very day she had been given to him, he asked her, "Are you really a poet?"

"Those who buy and sell me all say so," she replied.

He laughed and said, "Recite some of your poetry for us," and she recited the following verses:

The Right-Guided Ruler acceded
in the year three-and-thirty.
A caliphate entrusted to al-Mutawakkil[64]
when he was seven-and-twenty.
Let us hope, Right-Guided Ruler,
that your rule goes on for eighty.
God bless you! And on all who do not say "Amen"—
the curse of the Almighty!

Abū l-ʿAynāʾ said that the caliph liked the poem and gave her fifty thousand dirhams.

13.5 Via the same line of transmitters Abū l-Faraj al-Iṣfahānī cites Muḥammad ibn Khalaf,[65] who said that he heard Abū l-ʿAbbās al-Marwazī report the following:

Al-Mutawakkil said to ʿAlī ibn al-Jahm: "Recite a line of verse and tell Faḍl the Poetess to pick up where you leave off." So ʿAlī said: "Complete this rhyme, Faḍl:

He sought in her a sweet relief,
but found her bitter orange."[66]

She thought for a moment, and came back with:

He moaned and groaned and whined all night,
and creaked just like a door hinge.
She chewed him out, he died of love,
—and now I've met your challenge.

Al-Mutawakkil was delighted by this. "Well done, Faḍl, well done!" he cried, and ordered that she be given two thousand dirhams.

Via the same line of transmitters Abū l-Faraj al-Iṣfahānī relates that he heard Jaʿfar ibn Qudāmah report that Saʿīd ibn Ḥumayd reported the following: 13.6

I said to Faḍl the Poetess, "Cap this:

What help for one who loved in his youth?"

And, without missing a beat, she came back with:
A story told now that he's long in the tooth.

So I said:

A single glance made him sleepless and gaunt.[67]

And she came back with:

It all began with a glance, in truth!

Then after a moment's thought, she went on:

But for his hopes, he'd have died of grief
the long nights to his thoughts uncouth.
None was there to give relief,
on nights that dragged, or nights quick on the hoof.

Via the same line of transmitters, Abū l-Faraj al-Iṣfahānī relates: I read somewhere that Ibn al-Muʿtazz quotes the following story told by Ibrāhīm ibn al-Mudabbir: 13.7

Few in God's creation could match Faḍl the Poetess in elegance of handwriting, clarity of style, eloquence of expression, and in her ability to turn a phrase.

One day I said to Saʿīd ibn Ḥumayd, "I think you've been writing Faḍl's letters for her. Not to mention tutoring her and giving her tips on composition. That's why she sounds like you!"

"A nice thought!" he replied with a laugh. "If only she were getting it from me. No, in fact, I'm the one who's been imitating her style, and cribbing from her letters. My friend, if the most talented and senior state secretaries were to imitate her, by God, it would set a whole new standard!"

13.8 Abū ʿAlī al-Rāzī recited the following verses composed by Faḍl the Poetess:

My resolve weakens, my torment grows;
you are distant, though you live nearby.
Should I complain of you, or complain to you?
This wretched lover cannot decide.

13.9 Abū ʿAlī al-Naṭṭāḥah related the following story:

One night, as he was leaving a friend's house, a Hāshimī noticed a good-looking woman dressed in fine clothes in the midst of a group of women. He called out:

Those who go out after dark are suspect and shady

He said it loud enough for them all to hear. As quick as a wink, the woman in the middle of the group called back to him:

Except for the lover who yearns for his lady!

He asked who the woman was, and it turned out to be Faḍl the Poetess.

13.10 Muḥammad ibn Dāwūd ibn al-Jarrāḥ, in his book *The Folio: Accounts of the "Modern" Poets,* mentions her as follows:

Faḍl the Poetess, of the ʿAbd al-Qays tribe, was a dependent in the household of al-Mutawakkil. She was the most accomplished woman to write poetry in our time. Her poetry includes the following verses on daybreak:

The moon, so like you in beauty, my lord,
has driven away the darkness
Arise! Let's take our fill:
a nighttime drink,[68] *a kiss*
Before the sleepers' souls return
and expose us.

According to one historian, Faḍl the Poetess died in the year 257 [870–71]. 13.11

14

Bunān[69]

"Fragrances"

SLAVE OF THE CALIPH AL-MUTAWAKKIL

14.1 She was a poet and is mentioned by Abū l-Faraj al-Iṣfahānī in his *Book of Songs*.

14.2 I was informed by ʿAbd al-Raḥmān ibn Saʿd Allāh al-Daqīqī[70]—who cites Abū l-Qāsim ibn al-Samarqandī, citing Abū Manṣūr al-ʿUkbarī, citing Abū l-Ḥasan ibn al-Ṣalt, who cites Abū l-Faraj al-Iṣfahānī, who cites Jaʿfar ibn Qudāmah, who was told by Yaḥyā son of ʿAlī the astromancer, that he was told by al-Faḍl ibn al-ʿAbbās the Hāshimī—that Bunān the Poetess told al-Faḍl ibn al-ʿAbbās the following anecdote:

> One day, al-Mutawakkil went for a stroll in the palace courtyard,[71] with me on one arm and Faḍl the Poetess on the other. After taking a few steps, he quoted these lines:
>
> *Fearing she'd leave, I learned how to please her,*
> *but my love only taught her to revile.*
>
> "Cap that," he said, and Faḍl improvised:

He shrinks from my love, though I strive to come near,
to the warmth of my touch he is chill.

Then I added:

Whatever he does, my affection endures—
adore him I must and I will!

15

Maḥbūbah

"Beloved"

SLAVE OF THE CALIPH AL-MUTAWAKKIL

15.1 The author of *The Book of Songs* mentions her.

15.2 ʿAbd al-Raḥmān ibn Saʿd Allāh al-Daqīqī[72] informed me—citing Abū l-Qāsim ibn al-Samarqandī with permission, who cites Abū Manṣūr al-ʿUkbarī, citing Abū l-Ḥasan ibn al-Ṣalt—that Abū l-Faraj al-Iṣfahānī said:

> Maḥbūbah, the slave of al-Mutawakkil, was of mixed parentage. She was foremost of her generation both as a poet and as a singer. She had a beautiful face and voice.
>
> ʿUbayd Allāh ibn Ṭāhir gave her to al-Mutawakkil when he became caliph, as one of a group of four hundred slaves, some of them musically trained, others not. In his eyes, she surpassed them all.

15.3 Via the same transmitters, Abū l-Faraj al-Iṣfahānī relates that Jaʿfar ibn Qudāmah reported that Ibn Khurradādhbih reported that ʿAlī ibn al-Jahm said:

> I was once in the presence of al-Mutawakkil when he was drinking.[73] He handed Maḥbūbah an apple perfumed with

a scented musk blend.[74] She kissed it[75] and took her leave. Then one of her slaves appeared with a piece of paper which she handed to al-Mutawakkil. He read it, laughed, and tossed the paper to me to read. This is what it said:

You—fragrance of an apple I had to myself—
you ignite in me the fire of ecstasy.
I weep and complain of my malady,
and of my grief's intensity.
If an apple could weep, then the one I hold
would shed such tears of pity.
If you do not know what my soul has suffered
look, the proof is my body.
If you gaze upon it, you will see
one unable to suffer patiently.

Every single person present found these verses utterly delightful. Al-Mutawakkil ordered both ʿArīb and Shāriyah to set the verses to music, and those were the only songs sung the rest of the day.

Via the same transmitters, Abū l-Faraj al-Iṣfahānī relates that Jaʿfar 15.4
ibn Qudāmah reported that ʿAlī ibn Yaḥyā the astromancer said:

Al-Mutawakkil confided as follows to ʿAlī ibn al-Jahm, his close friend and confidant:

"I paid Qabīḥah the Poetess a visit and found that she had written my name on her cheek using a scented musk blend. I swear, ʿAlī, I've never seen anything more beautiful than that streak of black against her white cheek. Go ahead and compose a poem for me about that!"

Maḥbūbah was sitting behind the curtain, listening to us talk, and in the time it took for an inkstand and scroll of paper to be brought and for ʿAlī to formulate his thoughts, she had already improvised the following verses:

She wrote "Jaʿfar" in musk on her cheek,
how lovely that streak where the musk left its mark!

On her face she wrote just one line,
but she etched many more on my heart.
Who can help a master in thrall to his slave,
subservient in his heart, but plain to see,
Or one whose secret desire is Jaʿfar—
may he drink his fill from your lips![76]

ʿAlī ibn al-Jahm was dumbfounded at being upstaged like this. Al-Mutawakkil commanded ʿArīb to set the poem to music.

15.5 Via the same transmitters, I cite Abū l-Faraj al-Iṣfahānī, who relates that Jaʿfar ibn Qudāmah reported that ʿAlī ibn Yaḥyā the astromancer[77] reported the following to him, via ʿAlī ibn al-Jahm:

Al-Mutawakkil had a falling-out with Maḥbūbah and found it very hard to be apart from her. In the end, the pair made up.[78] Meanwhile I went to see him. He told me he'd had a dream that they had been reconciled, so he called a servant and said to him, "Go find out how she is and and see what she's doing."

The servant returned and told him that she was just singing.

"Can that woman really be singing when I'm so angry with her?" he said to me. "Come on, let's find out what she's crooning about."

We headed to her room, and she was singing:

I wander the palace, but I see no one,
no one will answer my plaint, it would seem.
I feel as though I've committed a sin,
one I can repent of but can never redeem.
Will someone plead my case to a king
who ended our quarrel when he came in a dream?
Yet when the dawn broke and the sun shone,
he forsook me again and left me alone.

Al-Mutawakkil was visibly moved. Realizing he was there, she came out of her room, and I made myself scarce.

She told him that she'd had a dream in which he'd come to her and they'd made up. That was why she had composed the poem, put it to music, and sung it. Al-Mutawakkil was so touched that he decided to stay and drink with her. She made sure I was well rewarded.

Via the same transmitters, Abū l-Faraj al-Iṣfahānī relates that ʿAlī ibn Yaḥyā the astromancer had reported to him that the slaves of al-Mutawakkil were divided up after his death. Several of them, including Maḥbūbah, ended up going to Waṣīf. 15.6

One day, as he was having his morning drink of wine, Waṣīf ordered that al-Mutawakkil's slaves be brought before him. They arrived in all their splendor, adorned, perfumed, and dressed in brightly colored clothes bedecked with jewels, except for Maḥbūbah, who came dressed in plain mourning white and not wearing any makeup.

The slaves sang, drank, and made merry, as did Waṣīf. Carried away by it all, he commanded Maḥbūbah to sing. She picked up the lute and sobbed as she sang:

What sweetness does life hold for me
when I cannot see Jaʿfar?
A king I saw with my own eyes
murdered, rolled in the dust.
The sick and the sorrowful,
they can all heal;
But not Maḥbūbah—
if she saw death for sale,
She would give everything she has to buy it
and join him in the grave.
For the bereaved,
death is sweeter than life.

The song struck home. Enraged, Waṣīf was on the point of having her killed, when Bughā, who happened to be present, said, "Give her to me!"

Bughā took her, gave her her freedom, and allowed her to live wherever she pleased. She left Samarra for Baghdad where she lived in obscurity and died of grief.

May God have mercy on her and reward her for her devotion to the memory of her beloved master!

16

Nāshib al-Mutawakkiliyyah

"Cupid"

MEMBER OF THE HOUSEHOLD OF THE CALIPH AL-MUTAWAKKIL

She was a singer renowned for her virtuosity and creative genius. 16.1
Judge Aḥmad ibn Kāmil transmitted literary material from her.

When I studied with master Abū ʿAbd Allāh al-Baghdādī, he dic- 16.2
tated this anecdote, which I read back to him:[79]

> I was told this in Cairo by ʿĪsā ibn ʿAbd al-ʿAzīz al-Lakhmī. He cites Aḥmad ibn Muḥammad al-Iṣfahānī, who cites al-Mubārak ibn ʿAbd al-Jabbār al-Ṣayrafī, who cites Abū Yaʿlā Aḥmad ibn ʿAbd al-Wāḥid the notary witness,[80] who in turn cites Abū l-Faraj al-Muʿāfā ibn Zakariyyāʾ, follower of al-Ṭabarī's school of legal thought, who was told by Judge Aḥmad ibn Kāmil:
>
> "I heard Nāshib al-Mutawakkiliyyah sing the following lines by Ibrāhīm ibn al-Mahdī:
>
> *You're wrong to accuse me,*
> *but slow to anger.*
> *Did I err? If so, then grant*
> *forgiveness as a favor."*

17

Fāṭimah

Daughter of al-Fatḥ ibn Khāqān

17.1 She was the wife of the caliph al-Mutawakkil's son al-Muʿtazz. Abū Ṭāhir al-Karkhī records that she died in the year 277 [890].

18

Farīdah

"Solitaire"

WIFE OF THE CALIPH AL-MUTAWAKKIL

This is the younger Farīdah.[81] Abū Bakr al-Ṣūlī mentions her, noting that Farīdah is correctly spelled with a long "i." 18.1

She was a slave who sang beautifully. In *The Book of Songs*, Abū l-Faraj al-Iṣfahānī credits her with setting to music the following verses by Abū l-ʿAtāhiyah: 18.2

Poor heart, stop beating!
How could life be any worse?
Will no one take my part?
My heart bears witness my love's bewitched me.
Before, when I was drunk with love,
I rushed to pleasure—my pants undone—
And the dark-eyed gazelle
pressed drinks on all my friends!

Farīdah belonged to the household of the caliph al-Wāthiq, who kept her as a concubine and favorite although she belonged to the singer ʿAmr ibn Bānah. When al-Wāthiq died, ʿAmr presented her to al-Wāthiq's brother al-Mutawakkil when he was given the oath 18.3

of allegiance as caliph. Al-Mutawakkil married her and she became one of his favorites.

Some say it was al-Wāthiq who received her from this same ʿAmr and that she subsequently became the property of al-Mutawakkil, who married her.

19

Nabt

"Flora"

SLAVE OF THE CALIPH AL-MUʿTAMID

Abū l-Faraj al-Iṣfahānī mentions her in *The Book of Songs*, where he writes: 19.1

> She was a singer with a beautiful voice and a poet with a gift for composing on the spot.

Aḥmad ibn al-Ṭayyib al-Sarakhsī quotes the following story from a state secretary: 19.2

> Nabt was shown to al-Muʿtamid, who tested her skill in singing and penmanship. He liked what he saw and said to Ibn Ḥamdūn, "Give her a half-line of poetry to cap." Ibn Ḥamdūn declaimed:
>
> *I gave my soul to love . . .*
>
> And she answered on the spot:
>
> *. . . and love ruled like a tyrant.*
>
> He continued:
>
> *So I became a humble slave . . .*

And she rejoined:

. . . and followed where he went.

Al-Muʿtamid ordered that she be bought. She fetched a price of thirty thousand dirhams.

19.3 I was informed by ʿAbd al-Raḥmān ibn Saʿd Allāh al-Daqīqī—who cited Abū l-Qāsim ibn al-Samarqandī, who cites Abū Manṣūr al-ʿUkbarī, citing Abū l-Ḥasan ibn al-Ṣalt, who cites Abū l-Faraj al-Iṣfahānī, citing Jaʿfar ibn Qudāmah—that Ibn Abī Ṭāhir said:

One day I went to see Nabt, Mukhfarānah the Ladyboy's slave.[82] She had a lovely face and a beautiful voice. I said to her, "I've composed a half-line for you to cap."

"Go ahead," she said, and I declaimed:

Nabt, your beauty outshines the moonlight . . .

She came back with:

. . . and your beauty all but robs me of my sight.

I paused to compose the next half-line but she beat me to it:

Your perfume is sweet as musk,
a breath from gardens in dawn's dim light.

I thought for a bit, but again she got in before me:

If you won't deign to make me yours
I'll not let you out of my sight.

Humiliated, I got up and left.

19.4 She was later presented to the caliph al-Muʿtamid who acquired her for thirty thousand dirhams on the advice of ʿAlī ibn Yaḥyā the astromancer.

20

Khallāfah

"Caprice"

Dependent of the Caliph al-Muʿtamid and Mother of His Son

She was one of al-Muʿtamid's favorites and highly esteemed. She had her own slave called Munyah, "Hope," the Scribe, about whom al-Khaṭīb al-Baghdādī[83] writes as follows in his *History*: 20.1

> Munyah cites material from Abū l-Ṭayyib Muḥammad ibn Isḥāq ibn Yaḥyā al-Washshāʾ, and ʿUbayd Allāh ibn al-Ḥusayn ibn ʿAbd Allāh al-Bazzāz al-Anbārī cites her.

21

Ḍirār

"Damage"

MOTHER OF THE CALIPH AL-MUʿTAḌID

21.1 She was the slave of the regent[84] al-Muwaffaq son of al-Mutawakkil, and enjoyed his favor. She bore him the future caliph al-Muʿtaḍid. Her name had formerly been Khafīr, "Bashful." She was always mindful of her dependents.

21.2 Ibn Abī Ṭāhir mentions her in his chronicle as follows:

> She died at the end of Jumada al-Awwal in the year 278 [early September, 891] and was buried in the Ruṣāfah Cemetery.

21.3 She did not live to see her son accede to the caliphate, as she passed away six days earlier. This is why I do not mention her in *The Lives of Those Gracious and Bounteous Consorts of Caliphs Who Lived to See Their Own Sons Become Caliph.*

22

Qaṭr al-Nadā[85]

Daughter of Khumārawayh son of Aḥmad ibn Ṭūlūn, whose real name was Asmā᾽

The caliph al-Muʿtaḍid married her by proxy while she was living with her father in Egypt. She arrived in Baghdad in the month of Rabiʿ al-Thani, 282 [June, 895]. Her dowry was so rich that it rivaled any royal treasury. She was one of the most intelligent and regal women who ever lived. 22.1

Abū l-Qāsim ʿAlī ibn ʿAbd al-Raḥmān recounted the following to me, citing Abū ʿAlī al-Bardānī, who quotes as his informant his brother Abū Ghālib Yūsuf ibn Muḥammad: 22.2

> Once when al-Muʿtaḍid's wife, the noble daughter of Aḥmad ibn Ṭūlūn, was mentioned, I heard my father say that al-Muʿtaḍid one day said to her:
>
> "You've done well for yourself by marrying the caliph! What more could you thank God for?"
>
> "You've done well for yourself," she retorted, "this makes my father your subject! What more could *you* thank God for?"[86]

Al-Ṭabarī states that Qaṭr al-Nadā lived with the caliph al-Muʿtaḍid until she passed away on the seventh of Rajab in the year 287 [July 8, 900]. She was buried in the precincts of the Caliphal Palace. 22.3

23

Khamrah

"Bouquet"

Dependent in the Household of the Caliph al-Muqtadir Son of al-Muʿtaḍid and the Mother of al-Muqtadir's Son ʿĪsā

23.1 Khamrah used to tell the following story, and her grandson, Prince Abū Muḥammad al-Ḥasan, the son of ʿĪsā, would retell it just the way she did. I heard it from master Abū ʿAbd Allāh al-Baghdādī, citing Abū l-Faraj al-Ḥarrānī, who cited Abū ʿAlī ibn Mahdī, who said: I heard Prince Abū Muḥammad, the grandson of al-Muqtadir, quote his father as saying, "My mother Khamrah, who was al-Muqtadir's slave, related as follows:

> Al-Muqtadir once called for some gemstones and picked out a hundred, fifty of which were spherical. He had them all strung as a rosary for his own use. The jewelers were asked to value it, and priced the stones at no less than a thousand dinars each.
>
> Whenever he wanted to tell his beads, he would send for this rosary. When he was done, he would hand it to me and I would put it in a jewelry bag and lock it in the strongbox.

> When looting broke out after al-Muqtadir's murder, it was one of the many things taken. I expect that whoever took it had no idea what it was."

The state secretary Hilāl ibn al-Muḥassin mentions in his *History*: 23.2

> Al-Muqtadir's slave Khamrah passed away on Tuesday the fifteenth of Rabiʿ al-Awwal in the year 378 [July 3, 988]. The bier of her son ʿĪsā was carried alongside hers. They were buried near the caliphal tombs[87] in the Ruṣāfah Cemetery.

She was always mindful of her obligations and performed many pious 23.3
deeds. She was generous to the poor, to the needy, to those who petitioned her, and to noble families who had fallen on hard times.

24

ʿIṣmah Khātūn[88]

Princess ʿIṣmah

Daughter of Sultan Malik-Shāh son of Sultan[89] Alp Arslān son of Dāwūd son of Mīkāʾīl son of Saljūq

24.1 She was a highly intelligent woman, an aristocrat and a virago. Her resolve was unswerving. The caliph al-Mustaẓhir—God be pleased with him—married her in Isfahan in the year 502 [1108–9]. She later came to Baghdad and took up residence in the Caliphal Palace.[90] She conceived, and on the second of Shaʿban in the year 505 [February 3, 1112] gave birth to Prince Abū Isḥāq Ibrāhīm; he died of smallpox during the month of Jumada al-Awwal, 508 [October, 1114], and was buried in the mausoleum of al-Muqtadir in al-Ruṣāfah, beside his uncle Jaʿfar, son of the caliph al-Muqtadī.

24.2 Upon the death of al-Mustaẓhir, ʿIṣmah Khātūn returned to Isfahan, where she passed away,[91] and was buried within the law college that she had founded there on Barracks Market Street. This was the biggest law college in the world. She endowed it for the followers of Abū Ḥanīfah—God show him mercy. I hear that nowadays it has become very run-down—it has no door and is uninhabitable.

25

Māh-i Mulk[92]

DAUGHTER OF SULTAN MALIK-SHĀH SON OF SULTAN ALP ARSLĀN SON OF DĀWŪD SON OF MĪKĀʾĪL SON OF SALJŪQ

In the month of Shawwal, 474 [March, 1082], the caliph al-Muqtadī sent Abū Naṣr ibn Jahīr to Māh-i Mulk's father in Isfahan to ask for her hand in marriage. Her father gave his consent and the marriage contract was concluded there and then. One hundred and forty camels and one hundred mules were needed to carry her belongings to Baghdad.[93] She arrived during the month of Dhu l-Hijjah, 479[94] [March, 1087]. The bridal procession and the consummation of the marriage took place in the month of Safar, 480 [May, 1087]. She conceived Prince Jaʿfar, and gave birth to him later that year, on the fourth of Dhu l-Qaʿdah [January 31, 1088]. But then the caliph began to avoid her and she asked permission to return home. She left Baghdad for Khurasan on the sixteenth of Rabiʿ al-Awwal in the year 482 [May 29, 1089], accompanied by her son, Prince Jaʿfar. 25.1

Subsequently, news of her death reached Baghdad. Her ailing father, Sultan Malik-Shāh, brought Prince Jaʿfar—his grandson and the caliph's son—back to Baghdad during the month of Ramadan, 25.2

485 [October, 1092]. A few days later, on the fifteenth of Shawwal [November 18, 1092], Malik-Shāh passed away. Prince Jaʿfar was taken back to the Caliphal Palace, where he remained until his own death on the twenty-third of Jumada al-Awwal in the year 486 [June 21, 1093]. The child was buried near the caliphal tombs in the Ruṣāfah Cemetery.[95]

26

Khātūn[96]

Princess

WIFE OF THE CALIPH AL-MUSTAẒHIR

She was one of al-Mustaẓhir's favorites. She passed away in the year 536 [1141–42]. Her palace was sacrosanct, for she and her retinue were held in great reverence. 26.1

27

Banafshā al-Rūmiyyah

"Amethyst" the Byzantine

DAUGHTER OF ʿABD ALLĀH,[97] DEPENDENT IN THE HOUSEHOLD OF THE CALIPH AL-MUSTAḌĪʾ—GOD BE PLEASED WITH HIM

27.1 The caliph held her in high regard and included her as part of his inner circle. She had authority and real power. She was also a godly, magnanimous woman who did all manner of good works and pious deeds. She looked after the poor and destitute and performed many righteous acts of charity. She converted her palace on the banks of the Tigris in Lower Baghdad into a Ḥanbalī law college and continually increased its endowment. She also had a stone bridge built over the ʿĪsā Canal and a pontoon bridge fixed across the Tigris.

27.2 The caliph al-Mustaḍīʾ built her a palace on the banks of the Tigris next to the Willow Gate of the Caliphal Palace. It was a lofty structure, with a spacious courtyard and numerous verandahs, apartments, belvederes, and promenades. The palace was adjacent to four waterwheels that brought water from the Tigris to the magnificent Caliphal Palace. Each wheel was positioned higher than the previous one, so that the first would take water from the Tigris, the second from the first, the third from the second, and the fourth from the third. When this palace was completed, Banafshā had a new pontoon bridge built connecting it to the Raqqah Gate on the West Side. This was put at the disposal of the general public and was a promenade for noble and commoner alike. I once heard the following verses declaimed about it:

Nothing measures up to the bridge's beauty:
a beauty unparalleled, without compare.
Banafshā has embroidered her name on the Tigris
an azure carpet, the bridge her signature.[98]

The palace was completed and fully furnished in the year 569 [1173–74]. Banafshā also built a large mosque in the Bakers' Market close to the Iron Archway.[99]

I have heard that every year on the Eid al-Fitr Festival she would donate the stipulated measure of dates to the needy and say, "This amount fulfills my religious obligation, but I hardly think it is enough for someone of my position." She would then donate an equivalent measure of gold coins to be distributed among the poor. She would also free a large number of slaves, both male and female. 27.3

She passed away on Friday the twenty-ninth of Rabiʿ al-Awwal in the year 598 [December 27, 1201]. Her funeral prayers were held in the Courtyard of Peace in the Caliphal Palace, following the late afternoon prayer. Her body was then carried by boat to the West Side and funeral prayers were again held for her at the gate to the mausoleum of the blessed consort, the mother of the caliph al-Nāṣir—God be pleased with him—which is adjacent to the mausoleum of Maʿrūf al-Karkhī—God have mercy on him. Banafshā was buried there even before the caliph al-Nāṣir's mother, for whom the mausoleum had been built, had herself passed away—God be pleased with her and her son.[100] 27.4

28

Sharaf Khātūn al-Turkiyyah

Lady "Honor" the Turk

MANUMITTED SLAVE OF THE CALIPH AL-MUSTAḌĪ', GOD BE PLEASED WITH HIM, AND MOTHER OF HIS SON PRINCE ABŪ MANṢŪR HĀSHIM

28.1 She was a devout woman. Her master, the caliph al-Mustaḍī', died during her lifetime, as did her son, Prince Abū Manṣūr, whom she long outlived.

She died the evening of Tuesday the nineteenth of Rajab in the year 608 [December 27, 1211]. Funeral prayers were held for her on Wednesday in the Courtyard of Peace, and she was buried in the Ruṣāfah Cemetery—God have mercy on her.

29

Saljūqī Khātūn

Princess Saljūqī

DAUGHTER OF QILIJ ARSLĀN[101] IBN MASʿŪD, RULER OF ANATOLIA, AND WIFE OF THE CALIPH AL-NĀṢIR, GOD BE PLEASED WITH HIM

She came to Baghdad on her way to perform the hajj in the pilgrimage season of the year 579 [1183–84] and returned home in 580 [1184–85]. Eighteen months later, the caliph al-Nāṣir of sacred memory sought her hand, and they were betrothed. He then sent an escort to bring her to Baghdad, consummated the marriage, and gave her priceless jewels and gifts fit for caliphs and kings. 29.1

She met with extraordinary favor on his part but only lived with him in the most comfortable and agreeable circumstances for a short time before death struck its sudden and untimely blow. She was plucked from a life of luxury and joined the ranks of the departed. Al-Nāṣir was so grief-stricken at her passing that he could not eat or drink for days. For many years her house was left just as it was, with all of its draperies and furnishings intact; it was never opened, nor was anything ever taken from it.

She had chosen to construct a mausoleum for herself at the Karkh landing on the West Side, beside the shrine of ʿAwn and Muʿīn, the 29.2.1

descendants of ʿAlī—peace be upon him.[102] Construction began, but before the walls were the height of a man, her time came, and it was only completed after her burial. A library of valuable books was installed there by bequest in perpetuity, to be lent against a deposit.

29.2.2 Next to her mausoleum, the caliph al-Nāṣir—God be pleased with him—built a splendid lodge with a large inner court which he endowed for the use of the Sufis. He had a pleasant orchard planted in front of it, overlooking the Tigris and irrigated by a waterwheel that drew from the river. He endowed many properties that generated produce and income to support both the Sufi lodge and her mausoleum.

He also arranged for someone to perform the hajj every year on her behalf; for quantities of alms to be handed out on the pilgrimage route to Mecca, including water, provisions, clothing, sandals, and medicine for the sick; and for a number of devout and virtuous persons to be sent on the hajj.

29.3 I read the following in the hand of Ibn al-Jawzī:[103]

> Saljūqī Khātūn, the wife of the caliph, died on the night of Monday the second of Rabiʿ al-Thani in the year 584 [May 31, 1188]. The funeral prayers were held for her in the Tāj Palace, and for three days condolences were received at her mausoleum. In attendance were the vizier, notables, commanders, and scholars, all of whom continued to pay their respects on Thursday nights and Sunday nights. Alms were distributed to the poor in her name. Everyone in the Caliphal Palace was genuinely grief-stricken. May God have mercy on her.

30

Shāhān

"Regina"

DEPENDENT IN THE HOUSEHOLD OF THE CALIPH AL-MUSTANṢIR OF SACRED MEMORY

She was a Byzantine slave belonging to Khatā Khātūn. Khatā Khātūn 30.1
was the daughter of the commander Sunqur al-Nāṣirī the Tall and the wife of the commander Jamāl al-Dīn Baklak al-Nāṣirī. Khatā Khātūn took such care of Shāhān's instruction and training, and showered her with so much attention, that everything about her suggested that she was destined for great things. When the caliph al-Mustanṣir was given the oath of allegiance, Khatā Khātūn presented Shāhān to him as a gift, as part of a group of slaves. Shāhān alone among them became his concubine and achieved a level of favor and intimacy that no one else could attain.

Shāhān went on to hold her own independent court and had a fiscal 30.2.1
office, agents, functionaries, servants, and a splendid retinue. She spent liberally from her funds just as she pleased, and her authority on all matters was unquestioned.

I was informed by one of her fiscal officials that she made a 30.2.2
monthly account of what was paid out to the tinsmiths, the weavers of embroidered cloth, the goldsmiths, the general merchants, the

cloth merchants, the jewelers, and the craftsmen of various types. The disbursement came to some one hundred and five thousand three hundred and sixty dinars.

30.3 She performed many pious acts of charity and was known for her attention to widows, orphans, and the poor, to whom she always gave alms. She was good, sought the good, and loved those who did good.

30.4.1 When Shāhān's master the caliph al-Mustanṣir passed away—God honor his grave and make Paradise his final resting place—he was succeeded by his son, Our Master the Commander of the Faithful, the caliph al-Mustaʿṣim—God support his noble and invincible reign and cause him to attain his desires in this world and the next. Al-Mustaʿṣim treated Shāhān with all the reverence, respect, and honor to which she was accustomed. He moved her—along with all her slave women, servants, retinue, and attendants—to the palace where she had been raised by her previous owner, Khatā Khātūn. It was known as Banafshā's Palace and was adjacent to the Willow Gate in the caliphal precinct. It was constructed for the caliphal consort Banafshā during the reign of al-Mustaḍīʾ, as I mentioned earlier.

30.4.2 When Khatā Khātūn was granted permission to reside in the palace, during the reign of the caliph al-Nāṣir—may God water those bygone days with the rain of divine mercy and pleasure—shops and houses were built nearby. A garden was laid out within it and all types of trees were transplanted there. It was always full of delicious fruits and beautiful flowers. The water was supplied by the waterwheels which irrigated the gardens of the Great Palace.

Facing this splendid palace is another stunning garden, filled with colorful fruit trees, creating a remarkable and breathtaking view. Anyone seated on its belvederes looks out over the Tigris and its pontoon bridge. It is a sight for sore eyes and a delight for the sorrowful heart.

The caliph also provided Shāhān with doormen, attendants, and footmen. She continued to receive from the Noble Treasury all the stipends and allowances she had received during the reign of al-Mustanṣir—may God water those bygone days with the rain of divine mercy and pleasure. An official notary was charged to remain at her door the entire day, ready to carry out her orders and to approve everything performed by the servants assigned exclusively to her.

Now that I have done as I promised and recorded the 30.5
consorts of caliphs, I move on to ones not yet mentioned,
namely consorts of commanders and viziers.

31

Dawlah

"Fortune"

SLAVE OF THE CALIPH IBN AL-MUʿTAZZ

31.1 She transmitted literary material from her master, Ibn al-Muʿtazz, and the grammarian Abū Bakr ibn al-ʿAllāf al-Shīrāzī transmitted material from her.

31.2 Master Abū ʿAbd Allāh al-Baghdādī informed me—citing Abū l-Qāsim al-Azajī, citing Abū l-Rajāʾ Aḥmad ibn Muḥammad al-Kisāʾī, quoting Abū Naṣr ʿAbd al-Karīm ibn Muḥammad al-Shīrāzī, who cites Judge Abū l-Faḍl Zayd ibn ʿAlī al-Rāzī, citing Abū ʿAlī al-Ḥusayn ibn Abī l-Qāsim al-Qāshānī—that Abū Bakr ibn al-ʿAllāf al-Shīrāzī said:

> Dawlah the slave of Ibn al-Muʿtazz recited this poem to us, which she said Ibn al-Muʿtazz had recited to her:[104]
>
> *I stood by the Euphrates:*
> *the boats were motionless in low water.*
> *Then I remembered you, tears flowed,*
> *and, as if driven by stormwinds, the boats sped by.*

32

Ḥayāt Khātūn

"Lady Life"

SLAVE OF THE CALIPH AL-ẒĀHIR—
MAY GOD BE PLEASED WITH HIM

She was a slave of Turkic origin, a favored and trusted concubine, 32.1
and the mother of one of his sons. She was manumitted upon his death and became a free woman.

She died on Friday the sixth of Safar in the year 639 [August 16, 1241], and funeral prayers were held for her in the Court of Peace. Her body was borne through the Bushrā Gate to the mausoleum of the caliph al-Mustaḍī' and buried there.

33

A CONSORT KNOWN BY REFERENCE TO ONE OF HER SERVANTS AS

Bāb Jawhar[105]

"Gate of Jewels"

33.1 She was a Turkic slave who was also a favorite of the caliph al-Ẓāhir. She was in his inner circle and had privileged access to him.

She died on the twenty-first of Muharram in the year 639 [August 1, 1241]. The majordomo of the Great Palace, Mu'ayyad al-Dīn Abū Ṭālib Muḥammad ibn al-ʿAlqamī, led the funeral prayers for her, and she was buried near the caliphal tombs in the Ruṣāfah Cemetery.

34

Qabīḥah

"Ugly"[106]

DEPENDENT IN THE HOUSEHOLD OF AL-ʿABBĀS IBN AL-ḤASAN, VIZIER TO THE CALIPH AL-MUQTADIR

She is the source for some of the verse of the poet Abū Bakr al-Ḥasan ibn al-ʿAllāf,[107] and Abū ʿAbd Allāh Muḥammad ibn al-Muʿallā transmits from her in his *Dictations*. 34.1

I read with master Abū ʿAbd Allāh al-Baghdādī—who cited Dhākir ibn Kāmil the shoemaker, who cited Abū Naṣr Maḥmūd ibn Faḍl al-Iṣfahānī as saying: it was related to us by Abū l-Qāsim al-Rabaʿī, who was informed by the supreme judge Abū l-Ḥasan al-Māwardī, citing Abū ʿAbd Allāh Muḥammad ibn al-Muʿallā in dictation—that Qabīḥah quoted this poem, which she heard from Abū Bakr al-Ḥasan ibn al-ʿAllāf himself: 34.2

Tell the one who bores the sick:
"If you visited a healthy man, you'd make him ill."
Do not sit long with him,
or his disease will lengthen and spread.
Just say hello and wish him well
and quickly leave the sufferer.

Visitors who overstay
aren't well-wishers, just insufferable.

34.3 Muḥammad ibn ʿAbd al-Wāḥid the Hāshimī related to me—citing Abū Muḥammad ʿAbd Allāh ibn al-Khashshāb,[108] citing al-Mubārak ibn ʿAbd al-Jabbār al-Ṣayrafī, who cited, with permission, the supreme judge Abū l-Ḥasan al-Māwardī, who quoted Abū ʿAbd Allāh Muḥammad ibn al-Muʿallā in dictation—saying that Qabīḥah quoted this poem which she heard from Abū Bakr al-Ḥasan ibn al-ʿAllāf:

It is as though you are in death's throes
your body about to depart.
Sped to your appointed time
after hopes false and deceptive.
Those you once protected
urge you now begone:
From hearse-bearers to corpse-washer
to pall-bearers, to the one who lays you in the grave.
Mortgaged to the House of Decay,
you gained a fleeting bargain.
You used to dwell, seen, above ground
now you dwell unseen beneath it.
You leave a sturdy house
for a dark, decrepit abode,
A house with living inmates,
for a house of the dead.
Let no man deceive himself:
woe to the self-deceived!

35

Sitt al-Nisā'[109]

Daughter of Ṭūlūn the Turk

She was extremely wealthy but also conspicuously munificent, prodigal, and openhanded. 35.1

When I studied with the Shāfiʿī notary witness Abū ʿAbd Allāh al-Baghdādī,[110] I said to him, "Didn't you study with the Ḥanbalī jurist Abū ʿAbd Allāh in Isfahan?" He confirmed that he had, and added: We learned the following from Abū l-Maḥāsin al-Jawharī, who reported that Ẓafar son of the ʿAlawī missionary quoted from his book citing Abū l-Ḥasan Muḥammad ibn al-Qāsim al-Fārisī, who cited Abū Naṣr al-Manṣūr ibn ʿAbd Allāh al-Iṣfahānī, saying he heard ʿAlī ibn ʿAbd al-Jabbār the Sufi say: 35.2

> Sitt al-Nisā', daughter of Ṭūlūn, married one of her dalliances and spent one hundred thousand dinars on her wedding banquet. Not long after, I saw her in the marketplace in Baghdad, reduced to begging. A rich man recognized her and asked, "Where are the comforts of your previous life?"
>
> "We expected the ravages of Fate to come lay waste to our lands—and so they did," she replied.
>
> "Is there any way I can help you now?" he asked.
>
> "Yes, fill my belly with food." she replied.

"Follow my agent home," he said, "and he will give you ten thousand dirhams."

"My brother," she said, "keep your money, and may God bless you. I once had far more, but it did not last." Sitt al-Nisā' then took something to eat, and said as she turned away:

Leave the world to its lovers,
soon to be its casualties.
Its praises are sung,
but I see its indignities.
Beware its seductive perfume:
its scent is lethal.
Its joys are poison,
its favors fatal.
How soon its eulogist
becomes its elegist.

36

Sarīrah al-Rāʾiqiyyah

"Secret"

SLAVE OF IBN RĀʾIQ

Thābit ibn Sinān mentions that she was dark-skinned, of mixed parentage, and that she sang beautifully. 36.1

She belonged to the daughter of the caliph's drinking companion, Ibn Ḥamdūn. The commander Abū Bakr Muḥammad ibn Rāʾiq purchased her from Ibn Ḥamdūn's daughter for thirteen thousand dirhams and Ibn Ḥamdūn took another thousand dinars from him as a brokerage fee. She gave Ibn Rāʾiq a son who did not survive, and Ibn Rāʾiq himself was killed while she was still in his possession. Then the Hamdanid Abū ʿAbd Allāh al-Ḥusayn ibn Saʿīd married her.

She died on Tuesday the thirteenth of Rajab in the year 348 [September 19, 959].

37

Khātūn al-Safariyyah

"Lady of Safar"[111]

37.1 She was the concubine of Sultan Malik-Shāh and bore him Muḥammad and Sanjar. She was exceedingly pious and regularly provisioned pilgrims on the route to Mecca.

37.2 She searched for her mother and her family till she found out where they lived, and paid someone a large sum to bring them to her. Her mother had not seen her for forty years; when she arrived, Khātūn surrounded herself with slaves who looked like her to see whether her mother would still recognize her. The moment she heard Khātūn speak, her mother sprang up, went to her, kissed her, and they embraced. The mother converted to Islam.

37.3 When Khātūn passed away, her stepson Sultan Maḥmūd received condolences for her.

37.4 She is one of those unusual women cited by historians as one of only four known to them to have given birth to either two caliphs or two kings:

To ʿAbd al-Malik, Wallādah daughter of al-ʿAbbās bore al-Walīd and Sulaymān, both of whom became caliph.

To al-Mahdī, al-Khayzurān bore al-Hādī and al-Rashīd, both of whom became caliph.

To al-Walīd, Shāh-i Āfrīd bore Yazīd and Ibrāhīm,[112] both of whom became caliph.

And to Malik-Shāh, this woman bore Muḥammad and Sanjar, both of whom became sultan.

38

Khātūn[113]

WIFE OF
SULTAN MALIK-SHĀH

38.1 She was the mother of Sultan Maḥmūd, whose father passed away while he was still a boy. He succeeded his father to the royal throne under the regency of his mother, who had in her service ten thousand Turkic slave soldiers. She directed the affairs of state and commanded the military until she passed away in the month of Ramadan, 487 [September, 1094]. When she died, Maḥmūd's rule became untenable. His own death followed soon thereafter, in the month of Shawwal of the same year [October, 1094].[114]

39

Zubaydah

Daughter of Berkyaruq and Wife of Sultan Mas‘ūd

She was lovely and praised for her beauty. She passed away in the year 532 [1137–38]. 39.1

Notes

1 Ḥammādah's father ʿĪsā ibn ʿAlī was the paternal uncle of the caliph al-Manṣūr.

2 The Arabic has *al-Ḥāfiẓ*, "the memorizer," meaning someone who has mastered one or more subjects.

3 The Arabic has a longer genealogy: Abū Sahl Aḥmad ibn Muḥammad ibn ʿAbd Allāh ibn Ziyād al-Qaṭṭān.

4 The Arabic has: Abū l-ʿAbbās Aḥmad ibn Yaḥyā Thaʿlab.

5 The caliph is asking Abū Dulāmah, a well-known poet, what elegy he has composed. Abū Dulāmah's answer shows him living up to his reputation as a jester.

6 The work from which Ibn al-Sāʿī is citing is not extant.

7 There are no missing or indistinguishable words but the meter makes clear that the verse is incomplete in the MS.

8 *Aḍghāth aḥlām* is an expression used in Q Yūsuf 12:44 («These are confusing dreams—we're unskilled at dream interpretation.») and in Anbiyāʾ 21:5 («Some say, "Muddled dreams!", and others say, "He has made it up."»). In the former, this is how Pharaoh's advisers characterize his dream, one which will later be correctly interpreted by the Prophet Joseph. In the latter, this is how some of the Prophet Muḥammad's interlocutors characterize the Qur'anic revelation.

9 The fact that ʿInān's father has no patronymic and that his given name, ʿAbd Allāh ("God's servant," a synonym of "Muslim"), was one quite often chosen by converts suggests that he may have been a convert.

10 His name appears as both al-Nāṭifī and al-Naṭṭāf in the entry; we have elected to use only al-Nāṭifī. The name means "seller of sweet nut brittle."

11 When a slave bears her owner a child, under the law she is supposed to be automatically manumitted upon his death.

12 Jinn were reckoned better poets than humans.

13 Verse 285 is the penultimate verse of Surah Baqarah. The surah has 286 verses, but liturgical recitation of the end of Surah Baqarah invariably consists of reciting both verses 285 and 286.

14 In his line, Abū Nuwās cleverly uses a Qur'anic verse with which Surah Baqarah finishes; ʿInān's verse is not only in the same meter and rhyme as his, as was expected, but also plays on the concept of "finishing" by using the verb *khatama* used to describe finishing a recitation of the entire Qur'an.

15 A reference to the Abbasid armies' summer campaigns.

16 The material from this point (f. 6a in the MS) through the end of §3.10 (both marked with asterisks), is incorrectly placed by the copyist in Bidʿah's entry (at §7.3, also marked with an asterisk). We have restored that material to ʿInān's entry, as does Jawād (see Ibn al-Sāʿī, *Nisāʾ al-khulafāʾ*, 51–53, 65).

17 The opening words of the line are slightly different in Jarīr's published *Dīwān*, 372.

18 We have not succeeded in replicating the paronomasia in the use of *ʿaliqa* and *ʿalūq* (both *ʿ-L-Q*) by Jarīr and *ʿaqala* (*ʿ-Q-L*) by ʿInān, though "hook" and "hocked" are an attempt to evoke this.

19 There is a lacuna here as ʿInān's response is not included in the manuscript. This is also precisely the end point of the material mistakenly placed in Bidʿah's entry (referred to in n. 16 above).

20 Al-Ṭabarī, *Tārīkh*, 759, has "Ghuṣaṣ" (غصص), not "Ghaḍīḍ" (غضيض), but al-Khaṭīb al-Baghdādī, *Tārīkh Baghdād*, 3:392, identifies her guardian as "al-Ghaḍīḍī," suggesting that "Ghaḍīḍ" is correct. Al-Ṭabarī also mistakenly has "Qaṣf" (قصف) for "Muṣaffā" (مصفى), which Bosworth corrects in al-Ṭabarī, *The ʿAbbāsid Caliphate in Equilibrium*, 352 (and cf. 328, n. 1103).

21 Or possibly "Helena," though the pet name which we render "Voilà" seems more likely. It is explained as a contraction of "Here she is now," which she would reportedly say whenever someone called her.

22 Four lines appear in al-ʿAbbās ibn al-Aḥnaf's extant *Dīwān*, 79.

23 The Arabic has Abū Aḥmad al-Amīn. We have standardized this to his given name, to match the reference in §1, for the convenience of the English reader.

24 The name of the younger al-Anbārī's father does not appear in the Arabic; we have supplied it.

25 This anecdote does not appear to be in any of al-Ṣūlī's extant works.

26 Or Banān ("Fingertips"); but see Kilpatrick, *Making the Great Book of Songs*, 328 and *passim*. Note that this is the male singer Bunān, not the female poet Bunān who is the subject of entry §14 below.

27 The description of the poet grieving at the departure of the tribe, and therefore the beloved, is one of the most famous topoi in Arabic poetry.

28 This is a quotation from the closing line of the song Bunān had sung earlier to the caliph.

29 This is Farīdah the Younger, the subject of entry §18 below.

30 She was bought and freed by al-Muʿtaṣim, thus "al-Maʾmūn's slave ʿArīb" (*ʿArīb jāriyat al-Maʾmūn*) here is merely an identification, not a description of her status when she died.

31 Or ninety-three years old by solar reckoning.

32 This is a very large sum.

33 Waṣīf was captured in ʿAyn Zarbah, near al-Maṣṣīṣah (modern-day Misis/Yakapınar), in Dhu l-Qaʿdah of 287 [November, 900]; al-Muʿtaḍid's first day back in Baghdad was the twenty-first of Dhu l-Hijjah in the year 287 [December 17, 900]: see al-Ṭabarī, *Tārīkh*, 2200, and al-Ṭabarī, *Return of the Caliphate to Baghdad*, 91.

34 An echo of Q Maryam 19:4 («my head blazes gray»).

35 Eggplant à la Būrān (or Eggplant Burani) is still a popular and widely available Iranian dish.

36 His name appears both as Thābit ibn Sinān ibn Qurrah and as Thābit ibn Qurrah. As several members of his family have the same name, we refer to him as Thābit ibn Sinān.

37 Bidʿah's funeral, the very last item reported by al-Ṭabarī in his *History*, is regrettably belittled as trivial by Rosenthal, the English translator, in al-Ṭabarī, *Return of the Caliphate*, 207, n. 978.

38 Al-Ḥasan ibn Sahl served al-Maʾmūn as secretary, general and governor, but never held the title of vizier; Ibn al-Sāʿī's use of the title here is honorific.

39 Būrān was only ten years old when they were married and eighteen when the marriage was consummated. See *EIran*, "Būrān."

40 An Abbasid prince who was dragged into political life by al-Maʾmūn's opponents and briefly proclaimed the anti-caliph. Al-Maʾmūn's forces captured and imprisoned him, but he was indeed later pardoned.

41 Wife of Hārūn al-Rashīd and mother of al-Amīn, who took her son's side against al-Maʾmūn; they were later reconciled.

42 A sleeveless surcoat, studded with large pearls, rubies, and other gems. See "jewel-studded surcoat" in the Glossary of Realia.

43 The Arabic here says "40 *mann*." The value of a *mann* varied between 700 and 850 g (see *EI2*, "Makāyil"); the candle thus weighed between 62 and 75 lbs. Since the number 70 is frequently approximate, it seemed appropriate to translate this as "seventy pounds."

44 This account does not appear in the extant part of al-Jahshiyārī's *Kitāb al-Wuzarāʾ wa-l-kuttāb*; Ibrāhīm Ṣālih includes it as a supplement to his 2009 edition.

45 The verb rendered as "strewed" is *nathara*, a term used to describe the showering of money and other valuables on joyous occasions, such as weddings and military victories. See §8.4 below and "bestowal" in the Glossary of Realia.

46 Hāshimī is the name given to anyone tracing descent from the Prophet Muḥammad, typically through his daughter Fāṭimah. The eponym, Hāshim, was Muḥammad's great-grandfather. Kisrā, from the Persian *Khusraw*, is a generic title applied to rulers of the Persian royal family, the Sassanids.

47 This is from Q Naḥl 16:1.

48 By this reckoning, she would have been born in 191/806, not 192/807.

49 The Arabic has "Madīnat al-salām," thus Baghdad, but the eastern part of Baghdad must be meant.

50 The Arabic has Muḥammad ibn ʿAbd Allāh. There is some uncertainty about Ibn al-Khashshāb's exact name in the sources, but the consensus is Abū Muḥammad ʿAbd Allāh, adopted here.

51 The manuscript has "Abū Jaz[z]" (أبو جز), which appears to be a copyist error. The conjectural al-Jammāz is based on the fact that this name appears in §3.10 above.

52 So named with reference to "The Eternal Paradise" of the Qur'an; see the glossary of places.

53 This anecdote does not appear in the extant volume of Ibn Abī Ṭāhir's *Kitāb Baghdād.*

54 According to Yāqūt, *Muʿjam al-buldān*, the Bīn Canal was also known as the Bīl Canal.

55 Al-Shammāsiyyah is a northeastern suburb of Baghdad, so al-Ma'mūn is not traveling far.

56 Al-Ṣūlī is clarifying that her name is "Farīdah" (فريدة), with a long "i", rather than "Farandah" (فرندة) with an "n." The undotted forms are identical.

57 Although al-Rabīʿ ibn Yūnus was indeed Hārūn's chamberlain, he held that position before Hārūn became caliph.

58 Isḥāq is a masculine name.

59 Faḍl is a masculine name.

60 That is, she is claiming descent from a "pure" Arab tribe.

61 The Rukhkhajī brothers were politically prominent.

62 That is to say, those listed in §13.2.1.

63 His paternal uncle, namely al-Ḥasan ibn Muḥammad.

64 The Arabic uses his given name, Jaʿfar.

65 Here for the first time he is cited in the Arabic by his fuller name: Muḥammad ibn Khalaf ibn al-Marzubān.

66 ʿAlī ibn al-Jahm uses an uncommon variant of a standard metrical form, something Faḍl's well-attuned ear catches, since she produces her response in the same variant. There is no "bitter orange" in the Arabic, nor a "door-hinge." We used "orange" as the rhyme word in order to try and convey the difficulty of the challenge posed by ʿAlī ibn al-Jahm.

67 At this juncture—as we have conveyed with the English too—Saʿīd ibn Ḥumayd does not retain the rhyme, though he does retain the meter. Faḍl nevertheless abides by the rhyme set by the original verse produced by Saʿīd.

68 She means wine.

69 Or Banān ("Fingertips"), as held e.g. by Jawād (in Ibn al-Sāʿī, *Nisāʾ al-khulafāʾ*, 91, n. 1).

70 The Arabic has ʿAbd al-Raḥmān al-Ṭaḥḥān. We have standardized this to ʿAbd al-Raḥmān ibn Saʿd Allāh al-Daqīqī to match the reference in §6.4, for the convenience of the English reader. Like al-Daqīqī, al-Ṭaḥḥān means "Flour Seller."

71 Probably the Hārūnī Palace built by al-Mutawakkil in Samarra on the banks of the Tigris.

72 We have replaced the origin name al-Wāsiṭī that appears in the Arabic with "al-Daqīqī." See n. 70 above.

73 Probably the Hārūnī Palace in Samarra.

74 This blend, *ghāliyah* (lit. "expensive"), was apparently so called because of its costly ingredients. See further the Glossary of Realia under "scented musk blend."

75 Preferring the reading *qabbalat-hā* (قبّلتها), "she kissed it," to the manuscript's *qallabat-hā* (قلّبتها), "she turned (or looked) it over."

76 Jaʿfar is not only the caliph al-Mutawakkil's given name, but also a word that means "river" or "stream." Maḥbūbah's desire to be given something to drink by/from *jaʿfar* is thus a play on words. We have rendered it "drink . . . from your lips."

77 The Arabic has *mawlāya*, "my patron"; as ʿAlī ibn Yaḥyā is undoubtedly meant we have used his name here.

78 The Arabic has صالحه, third-person masculine. We emend it, reading it as third-person feminine صالحته. Alternatively, one could read the latter as first-person صالحتُه: this would give, "I tried to reconcile them and then went to see him."

79 One important method of scholarly transmission was for students to write down the teacher's words and then read this back to the teacher for verification.

80 A person regularly engaged by a judge as a witness to contractual obligations or to the character of persons appearing in court.

81 For the older Farīdah, see §11 above. For the point about the spelling of the name, see n. 56.

82 On transvestism, see Rowson, "Gender Irregularity."

83 In the Arabic, the name appears as Abū Bakr Aḥmad ibn Thābit al-Khaṭīb. The "al-Khaṭīb" in his name is not an honorary title or a reference to a forebear: he was in fact a *khaṭīb*, a man who gave Friday sermons.

84 The Arabic has Imām as his title. This title is usually reserved for caliphs, whereas al-Muwaffaq was regent, which is how we have rendered it.

85 Qaṭr al-Nadā is a nickname meaning "Dewdrop," but she is not a slave.

86 The caliph's point is that Qaṭr al-Nadā should be grateful for an alliance that has wed her, the daughter of a provincial governor, to the caliph himself, and her point is that he should be grateful that her father, a potentate in his own right, has now returned, through his daughter's marriage, to the caliphal fold.

87 The Arabic has "honorable tombs" (*al-turab al-sharīfah*), a characterization that recurs in §25.2 and §33.

88 Khātūn is a title (of Soghdian origin) borne by the wives and female relatives of high-ranking Saljūqs. The name ʿIṣmah means, among other things, "modesty."

89 "Sultan" does not appear before Alp Arslān's name in the Arabic, but does so in the next entry; we have accordingly added it here to be consistent.

90 This was two years later, in 504/1010–11.

91 Al-Mustaẓhir died in 512/1118 and ʿIṣmah Khātūn in 536/1141–42.

92 Māh-i Mulk, also called Muh Malak and Malik Khātūn.

93 There is dittography of the number four hundred. Other accounts record different numbers of camels and mules. This represents the best reconstruction.

94 The Arabic truncates the date 479 to '79 here, and later also 480 to '80 and 482 to '82: we use the expanded forms.

95 He was five years old.

96 This is the same person as ʿIṣmah Khātūn (§24 above). The confusion is evidence of the fact that the latter part of *Consorts of the Caliphs* was still a work in progress and in draft form.

97 *Banafshā* is also "Violet." Her father may have been a convert to Islam: he has no patronymic, and his name, ʿAbd Allāh, "God's servant," a synonym of "Muslim," was quite often chosen by converts. See n. 9.

98 Banafshā's name is reported to have been carved on the bridge; the poem likens it to *ṭirāz* embroidery (see Glossary of Realia).

99 See Makdisi, "Topography of Baghdad." The Iron Archway was sometimes known as the New Archway and might conceivably be meant here instead (Iron: حديد; New: جديد), but as the Bakers' Market appears to be further west, this does seem to be an iron archway, of which there were several.

100 Al-Nāṣir's mother, Zumurrud Khātūn, was a Turkic slave. She too endowed buildings for use by the Ḥanbalīs in Baghdad.

101 Properly, Kılıc Arslan.

102 The pious phrase after ʿAlī ibn Abī Ṭālib's name is usually "may God be pleased with him" (*raḍiya Allāh ʿanhu*). The use of "peace be upon him" (*ʿalayhi l-salām*) is unusual, but not unheard of; it is routinely used after ʿAlī's name by Shiʿites, for instance.

103 This is likely from Ibn al-Jawzī's *Durrat al-iklīl*, which covered the years 574–90/1178–94. See Ibn al-Jawzī, *al-Muntaẓam*, 18:255, n. 2.

104 These verses do not appear in the extant *Dīwān* of Ibn al-Muʿtazz.

105 The sources do not pronounce on the precise meaning of the name.

106 Although *Qabīḥah* means "ugly," she was probably quite beautiful. It was not uncommon to give someone a name with the opposite meaning, either ironically or to ward off the evil eye. Cf. her namesake, mentioned in §15.4 above.

107 Not the grammarian Ibn al-ʿAllāf cited in §31 above.

108 Cf. n. 50 above.

109 Her name means "[Noble] Lady among women" or "Queen among women."

110 The Arabic has Muḥammad ibn Maḥmūd here, perhaps to avoid the confusion of two consecutive scholars called Abū ʿAbd Allāh.

111 A town in Khwārazm, though the geographical sources do not specify precisely where.

112 Scholarly consensus is that Ibrāhīm's mother was not Shāh-i Āfrīd, the granddaughter of Yazdagird III, but rather the slave Suʿār.

113 Her given name was Terken, but it is not mentioned by Ibn al-Sāʿī.

114 Maḥmūd was only four years old when his mother placed him on the throne. She was put to death; Maḥmūd died of illness soon after her.

The Abbasid Caliphs

- ʿAbd al-Muṭṭalib
  - ʿAbd Allāh
    - Prophet Muḥammad
  - al-ʿAbbās
    - ʿAbd Allāh
      - ʿAlī
        - Muḥammad
          - 1. Abū l-ʿAbbās al-Saffāḥ 133–37/750–54
          - 2. Abū Jaʿfar al-Manṣūr 137–59/754–75
            - 3. al-Mahdī 159–69/775–85
              - 4. al-Hādī 169–70/785–86
              - 5. Hārūn al-Rashīd 170–94/786–809
                - 6. al-Amīn 194–98/809–13
                - 7. al-Maʾmūn 198–218/813–33
                - 8. al-Muʿtaṣim 218–28/833–42
                  - 10. al-Mutawakkil 233–47/847–61
                    - 11. al-Muntaṣir 247–48/861–62
                    - 13. al-Muʿtazz 252–56/866–69
                    - 15. al-Muʿtamid 257–79/870–92
                    - al-Muwaffaq
                  - 9. al-Wāthiq 228–33/842–47
                    - 14. al-Muhtadī 256–57/869–70
                  - Muḥammad
                    - 12. al-Mustaʿīn 248–52/862–66

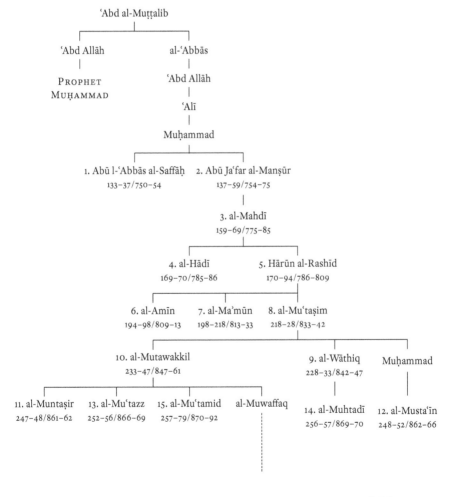

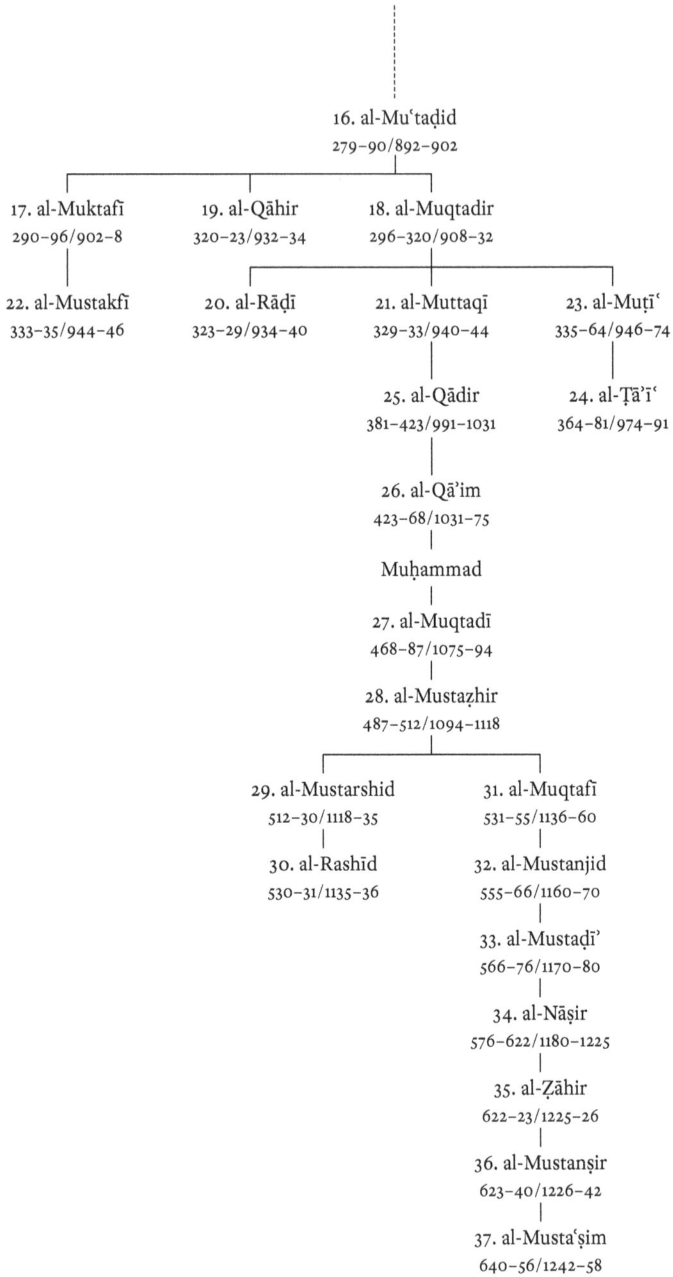
16. al-Muʿtaḍid
279–90/892–902
17. al-Muktafī
290–96/902–8
19. al-Qāhir
320–23/932–34
18. al-Muqtadir
296–320/908–32
22. al-Mustakfī
333–35/944–46
20. al-Rāḍī
323–29/934–40
21. al-Muttaqī
329–33/940–44
23. al-Muṭīʿ
335–64/946–74
25. al-Qādir
381–423/991–1031
24. al-Ṭāʾīʿ
364–81/974–91
26. al-Qāʾim
423–68/1031–75
Muḥammad
27. al-Muqtadī
468–87/1075–94
28. al-Mustaẓhir
487–512/1094–1118
29. al-Mustarshid
512–30/1118–35
31. al-Muqtafī
531–55/1136–60
30. al-Rashīd
530–31/1135–36
32. al-Mustanjid
555–66/1160–70
33. al-Mustaḍīʾ
566–76/1170–80
34. al-Nāṣir
576–622/1180–1225
35. al-Ẓāhir
622–23/1225–26
36. al-Mustanṣir
623–40/1226–42
37. al-Mustaʿṣim
640–56/1242–58

The Early Saljūqs

Saljūq

Mīkā'īl

1a. Ṭughril
431–55/1040–63

1b. Dāwūd
431–52/1040–60

2. Alp Arslān
455–65/1063–72

3. Malik-Shāh I
465–85/1072–92

4. Maḥmūd
485–87/1092–94

5. Berkyaruq
487–98/1094–1105

6. Malik-Shāh II
498/1105

7. Muḥammad I
498–511/1105–18

8. Sanjar
511–52/1118–57

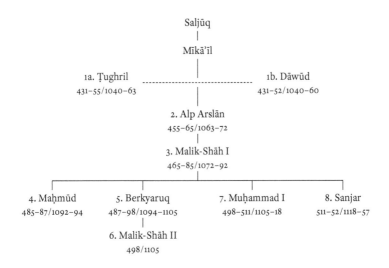

Chronology of Women Featured in *Consorts of the Caliphs*

Note: An interrogation mark is used when a death date is not known, and relative placement represents educated conjecture.

INDIVIDUAL	DATE OF DEATH	
	Hijri	*Gregorian*
Ḥammādah (§1)	164	780–81
Ghādir (§2)	173	789–90
Haylānah (§5)	173	789–90
Ghaḍīḍ (§4)	193	809
ʿInān (§3)	226	840–41
Faḍl al-Shāʿirah (§13)	257	870–71
Mu'nisah (§9)	?	?
Farīdah (the Elder) (§11)	?	?
Bunān (§14)	?	?
Farīdah (the Younger) (§18)	?	?
Nabt (§19)	?	?
Isḥāq al-Andalusiyyah (§12)	270	883
Būrān (§8)	271	884
ʿArīb (§6)	277	890
Fāṭimah (§17)	277	890
Ḍirār (§21)	278	891

INDIVIDUAL	DATE OF DEATH	
	Hijri	*Gregorian*
Qurrat al-ʿAyn (§10)	?	?
Maḥbūbah (§15)	?	?
Qaṭr al-Nadā (§22)	287	900
Bidʿah (§7)	302	915
Nāshib (§16)	?	?
Khallāfah (§20)	?	?
Dawlah (§31)	?	?
Qabīḥah (§34)	?	?
Sitt al-Nisāʾ (§35)	?	?
Sarīrah (§36)	348	959
Khamrah (§23)	378	988
Khātūn al-Safariyyah (§37)	466	1073–74
Māh-i Mulk (§25)	ca. 484	ca. 1091
[Terken] Khātūn (§38)	487	1094
Zubaydah (§39)	532	1137–38
ʿIsmah Khātūn (§24)	536	1141–42
Khātūn (§26) = ʿIsmah Khātūn		
Saljūqī Khātūn (§29)	584	1188
Banafshā (§27)	598	1201
Sharaf Khātūn (§28)	608	1211
Bāb Jawhar (§33)	639	1241
Ḥayāt Khātūn (§32)	639	1241
Shāhān (§30)	652	1254–55

Glossary of Names

Note: Individuals are listed according to the way we have rendered the names in the translation. When we include other parts of the name, this reflects Ibn al-Sāʿī's usage. We occasionally supply other parts of the name in the gloss. Transliteration follows the conventions of *EI3*. Note the following differences between the conventions of *EI2* and *EI3*: *EI2* uses dj instead of j, and ḳ instead of q; thus, for instance, one would search for Saldjūḳ in *EI2*, but Saljūq in *EI3*. Turkic names are also differently rendered: thus, Barkyāruḳ in *EI2* but Berkyaruq in *EI3*.

Characters

Abān al-Lāḥiqī (§3.8) (d. ca. 200/815) Poet of the early Abbasid period born into a family of Jewish ancestry in Basra, patronized by the Barmakids. He made a name for himself writing panegyrics, versifications of prose works from the Persian and Indic traditions, and lampoons.

al-ʿAbbās ibn al-Aḥnaf (§5) (d. ca. 192/807) Leading early love poet at the Abbasid court and a favorite of Hārūn al-Rashīd, whom he apparently accompanied on military campaigns. His poetry was highly regarded and frequently set to music. He composed an elegy on **Haylānah** (§5).

al-ʿAbbās ibn al-Ḥasan (§34) (d. 296/909) Al-Jarjarāʾī, vizier of the caliphs al-Muktafī and al-Muqtadir. He was killed by a partisan of the short-lived caliph Ibn al-Muʿtazz. **Qabīḥah** (§34) was a dependent in his household.

ʿal-Abbās ibn Rustam (§3.8) (fl. second/eighth c.) Associate of the poet Abān al-Lāḥiqī.

ʿAbbāsah (§4) (d. early to mid-third/ninth c.) Abbasid princess, daughter of al-Mahdī, half-sister of Hārūn al-Rashīd and Ibrāhīm ibn al-Mahdī. Her supposed marriage to Jaʿfar ibn Yaḥyā the Barmakid was popularly believed to have been the cause of the rift between Hārūn and Jaʿfar that led to the Barmakid downfall.

Abbasids Dynasty of caliphs that ruled the Islamic empire 132–656/750–1258. Their capital, Baghdad, was founded by the caliph al-Manṣūr in 145/762.

ʿAbd Allāh (§3) (fl. second/eighth c.) The father of ʿ**Inān** (§3). Judging by his generic given name he was likely a convert to Islam.

ʿAbd Allāh (§11) (fl. third/ninth c.) Son of **Farīdah** al-Amīniyyah (§11) and al-Haytham ibn Bassām.

ʿAbd Allāh (§27) (fl. sixth/twelfth c.) The father of **Banafshā** (§27). Judging by his generic given name he was likely a convert to Islam.

ʿAbd al-Qays (§§13.2.2, 13.10) Old East Arabian tribe.

Abū ʿAbd Allāh al-Ḥusayn ibn Saʿīd ibn Ḥamdān (§36) (fl. fourth/tenth c.) Scion of the Hamdanids, a family in Abbasid service before they established their own dynasty in the third/ninth and fourth/tenth centuries in northern Iraq and Syria. **Sarīrah** (§36) was married to Abū ʿAbd Allāh.

Abū Aḥmad al-Muwaffaq See al-Muwaffaq.

Abū ʿAlī al-Naṭṭāḥah (§13.9) (d. after 300/913) State secretary and litterateur. Some of his poetry and a large quantity of his prose, principally epistolary to Ibn al-Muʿtazz and others, survives.

Abū l-ʿAtāhiyah (§18.2) (d. ca. 210/825) Major court poet of modest beginnings. He wrote love poems about ʿUtbah, a slave belonging to the caliph al-Mahdī's cousin, and became famous for ascetic verse. Many of his poems were put to music.

Abū l-ʿAynāʾ (§§3.8, 3.10, 8.8.2, 8.8.3, 13.4) (d. ca. 282/896) Litterateur and poet originally from Basra, known for his repartee and quick wit. He became blind at the age of forty. Ibn Abī Ṭāhir compiled a book of anecdotes concerning him, many of which are quoted by Abū l-Faraj al-Iṣfahānī.

Abū Bakr (§7.6) (fl. late third/ninth to early fourth/tenth c.) Son of the caliph al-Muhtadī, but not selected to be his successor. He was at court in 302/915, as he led the funeral prayer for **Bidʿah** al-Kabīrah (§7).

Abū Bakr Muḥammad ibn Rāʾiq (§36) See Ibn Rāʾiq.

Abū Dulaf al-Qāsim ibn ʿĪsā al-ʿIjlī (§13.3) (d. between 225/840 and 228/843) Poet, musician, litterateur, military commander under the caliph al-Amīn, and governor under the caliph al-Muʿtaṣim.

Abū Ḥanīfah (§24.2) (d. 150/767) Jurist, theologian, and eponym of the Ḥanafī school of legal thought, favored by the early Abbasids. He may have had a hand in planning the construction of the city of Baghdad.

Abū Isḥāq Ibrāhīm (§24.1) (d. 508/1114) Abbasid prince, son of the caliph al-Mustaẓhir and ʿ**Iṣmah Khātūn** (§24) daughter of Malik-Shāh; he died of smallpox at the age of two and was buried next to Prince Abū l-Faḍl Jaʿfar in the Ruṣāfah Cemetery.

Abū Jaʿfar ʿAbd Allāh al-Manṣūr (§1) See al-Manṣūr.

Abū Jaʿfar al-Manṣūr al-Mustanṣir bi-llāh (§§30, 30.1, 30.4.1, 30.4.2) See al-Mustanṣir.

Abū Manṣūr Hāshim (§28) (fl. sixth/twelfth c.) Abbasid prince, son of the caliph al-Mustaḍīʾ and **Sharaf Khātūn** (§28).

Abū Muḥammad al-Ḥasan ibn ʿĪsā (§23.1) (d. 378/988) Grandson of the caliph al-Muqtadir and **Khamrah** (§23).

Abū Naṣr ibn Jahīr (§25.1) (d. 483/1090) Founding member of the politically active Jahīr family who all but monopolized the vizierate during the protectorate of the Great Saljūqs, i.e. starting in 454/1062, when Abū Naṣr assumed the position, and continuing for the next five decades.

Abū Nuwās (§§3.7, 3.10, 8.4) (d. ca. 198/813) Celebrated Abbasid poet, confidant and court companion of the caliph al-Amīn. He was highly accomplished and versatile. The genres in which he excelled included wine poetry (*khamriyyāt*), hunting poetry (*ṭardiyyāt*), and love poetry addressed to both men and women.

Aḥmad ibn Ṭūlūn (§22.2) (r. 254–70/868–84) Son of a male slave given to al-Maʾmūn by the governor of Bukhara. The caliph al-Muʿtazz appointed him governor of Egypt, which he ruled autonomously, establishing the Tulunids as a dynasty. The mosque he built in Cairo in 259/872 still stands.

Aḥmad ibn Yūsuf (§9) (d. 213/828) Private secretary to al-Ma'mūn, and one of his intimates, he came from a family of secretaries and scribes from Kufa. By virtue of his aphorisms in prose and in verse, he has come to be regarded as a "secretary-poet," a typically "modern" (*muḥdath*) type of amateur man of letters.

ʿAlī ibn al-Jahm (§§13.5, 15.3–15.5) (d. 249/863) Prominent Abbasid poet and litterateur. He was close to the caliph al-Mutawakkil but jealous courtiers caused him to be exiled to Khurasan. Among his famous poems is an elegy to al-Mutawakkil.

ʿAlī ibn Sahl ibn Abān (§8.3.3) (fl. third/ninth c.) A dependent of al-Ḥasan ibn Sahl.

ʿAlī ibn Yaḥyā the astromancer (§§6.5, 7.2, 12.3, 15.4, 15.5, 15.6, 19.4) (d. 275/888) Prominent courtier, poet, musician, and man of learning from the al-Munajjim family of caliphal companions and astromancers. He was a companion to a succession of caliphs and an important patron of writers and poets at his family estate, where he amassed an impressive library; he also put together a library for the caliph al-Mutawakkil's secretary, al-Fatḥ ibn Khāqān.

Alp Arslān (§§24, 25) (r. 455–65/1063–72) Saljūq Sultan. He focused largely on military campaigns, leaving the administration of empire to his famous vizier, Niẓām al-Mulk.

al-Amīn (§§6.1, 8.10, 11) (d. 198/813) Regnal title of Muḥammad ibn al-Rashīd; he succeeded his father Hārūn al-Rashīd as caliph. He was killed in the Civil War with his brother al-Ma'mūn, who then assumed the caliphate.

ʿAmr ibn Bānah (§18.3) (d. 279/892) Son of a government scribe, a singer during the caliphate of al-Ma'mūn and his immediate successors, and author of two songbooks. He was the owner of **Farīdah** (§18), whom he presented to the caliph al-Mutawakkil (or possibly the caliph al-Wāthiq).

ʿArafah (§7.3–7.5) (fl. third/ninth c.) Legal representative of **Bidʿah al-Kabīrah** (§7) and handler of her affairs.

ʿArīb al-Maʾmūniyyah *(§6; §§7.2, 7.6, 15.3, 15.4)* (d. 277/890) The most famous female musician of the third/ninth century. She was sold by her Christian wet nurse to a slave trader and bought by the caliph Hārūn al-Rashīd's boatmaster, who raised and educated her. She maintained that she was the daughter of Jaʿfar the Barmakid. She was owned by the caliphs al-Amīn and al-Maʾmūn, bought and freed by the caliph al-Muʿtaṣim, and had liaisons with numerous caliphs.

Bāb Jawhar *(§33)* (d. 639/1241) Turkic slave who was a favorite of the caliph al-Ẓāhir.

Banafshā al-Rūmiyyah *(§27; §30.4.1)* (d. 598/1201) Wife of the caliph al-Mustaḍīʾ, a very pious woman who engaged in many acts of charity and who was an important patron of the Ḥanbalīs, for whom she endowed a law college. See Map 4.

Barmakids (§§6.1, 6.2, 8.8.4, 11) A family of viziers and administrators, originally Buddhists from Balkh, who served the first five Abbasid caliphs. Yaḥyā ibn Khālid ibn Barmak, foster father and tutor to the future Hārūn al-Rashīd, was an extremely important patron of poetry and scholarship. For reasons that remain unknown, Hārūn al-Rashīd deposed the Barmakids in 187/803, imprisoning and executing many of them.

Berkyaruq (§39) (r. 487–98/1094–1105) Saljūq sultan, the son of Malik-Shāh. His reign included confrontations regarding succession with Terken (see **Khātūn** §38), Malik-Shāh's wife, who seized power on behalf of her infant son Maḥmūd ibn Malik-Shāh.

Bidʿah *(al-Kabīrah) (§7)* (d. 302/915) Slave belonging to ʿ**Arīb** (§6), a dependent in the household of the caliph al-Maʾmūn, and reputed to be the best and most beautiful singer of her time. She was admired by al-Muʿtaḍid.

Bughā (al-Ṣaghīr or al-Sharābī) (§15.6) (d. 254/868) Abbasid commander, close collaborator of Waṣīf al-Turkī, very likely a member of the Samarra-based Turkic military slave corps. He likely had a hand in—or even organized—the assassination of the caliph al-Mutawakkil and the civil war in Baghdad in 251/865.

Bunān (or Banān) (§6.5) (fl. third/ninth c.) Male singer who performed for several caliphs including al-Mutawakkil, al-Muntaṣir, al-Muʿtazz, and al-Muʿtamid and who had an affair with **Faḍl al-Shāʿirah** (§13).

Bunān (or Banān) (§14) Slave of al-Mutawakkil; a poet mentioned by Abū l-Faraj al-Iṣfahānī in the *Book of Songs*.

Būrān (§8; §§6.6, 7.5) (d. 271/884) Her given name was Khadījah; she was the daughter of al-Ḥasan ibn Sahl, the caliph al-Maʾmūn's deputy in Iraq. She was betrothed to al-Maʾmūn at a young age, was married to him when she was eighteen, and long outlived him.

Dawlah (§31) (fl. late third/ninth c.) Slave of the caliph Ibn al-Muʿtazz, a transmitter of literary material, and a poet in her own right.

Ḍirār (§21) (d. 278/891) Slave of the regent al-Muwaffaq; she bore him the future caliph al-Muʿtaḍid.

al-Faḍl ibn Yaḥyā (§6.2) (d. 193/808) Son of Yaḥyā the Barmakid and brother of Jaʿfar ibn Yaḥyā, influential in the court of the caliph Hārūn al-Rashīd and tutor there to the crown prince al-Amīn. His political views may have contributed to the downfall of the Barmakids. He was imprisoned in 187/803 and died some years later.

Faḍl al-Shāʿirah (§13; §14.2) (d. ca. 257/870–71) "Faḍl the Poetess," slave of the caliph al-Mutawakkil, one of the most accomplished poets, women of letters, and wits of her time.

Farīdah (§18; §6.7) Slave who belonged to the singer ʿAmr ibn Bānah but whom the caliph al-Wāthiq kept as a concubine. When al-Wāthiq died, ʿAmr gave her to al-Mutawakkil (or she may have belonged to al-Wāthiq). Al-Mutawakkil married her.

Farīdah al-Amīniyyah (§11) Slave of mixed parentage who grew up in the Hijaz. She belonged successively to al-Rabīʿ ibn Yūnus, the Barmakids, and the caliph al-Amīn. She fled after al-Amīn's death and married al-Haytham ibn Bassām and, later, al-Sindī ibn al-Ḥarashī.

Fāṭimah (§17) (d. 277/890) Daughter of the Turkic courtier, diplomat, and commander al-Fatḥ ibn Khāqān; she was the wife of the caliph al-Mutawakkil's son, al-Muʿtazz, who later became caliph.

Ghaḍīḍ (§4) (d. before 193/809) Slave of the caliph Hārūn al-Rashīd and mother of his daughter Ḥamdūnah.

Ghādir *(§2)* (d. before 173/789–90) Slave of the caliph al-Hādī, who married Hārūn al-Rashīd on al-Hādī's death.

al-Hādī (§§2.1.1, 37.4) (r. 169–70/785–86) Fourth Abbasid caliph, son of the caliph al-Mahdī. He was hostile to his brother Hārūn, whom he imprisoned, but who succeeded him when he died suddenly. Hārūn then married al-Hādī's favorite **Ghādir** (§2).

Ḥamdūnah (§4) (fl. early third/ninth c.) Daughter of the caliph Hārūn al-Rashīd with **Ghaḍīḍ** (§4).

Ḥammādah bint ʿĪsā *(§1)* (d. 164/780–81) Daughter of ʿIsā, the paternal uncle of the caliphs al-Saffāḥ and al-Manṣūr. She was married to al-Manṣūr.

Ḥanbalī (§§27.1, 35.2) Member of the school of legal thought named for Aḥmad ibn Ḥanbal (d. 241/855). Ḥanbalīs and Ḥanbalism were favored by several ladies of the later Abbasid dynasty.

Hārūn al-Rashīd (§§2.1, 2.2, 3.2, 4, 5, 6.1, 6.2, 8.8.4, 8.10, 11, 37.4) (r. 170–93/786–809) Fifth Abbasid caliph, son of the caliph al-Mahdī and al-Khayzurān, a slave from Yemen whom al-Mahdī freed and married. Hārūn's wives included his cousin Zubaydah, **Ghādir** (§2), and later **Ghaḍīḍ** (§4), who bore him a daughter, Ḥamdūnah.

al-Ḥasan ibn Sahl (§§8, 8.3.1, 8.3.2, 8.4, 8.8.1, 8.10, 8.11) (d. 235/850) Zoroastrian convert to Islam employed by al-Faḍl ibn Yaḥyā the Barmakid. Al-Ḥasan's daughter **Būrān** (§8) was married to the caliph al-Maʾmūn, whom her father served as a high official. Al-Maʾmūn gave him the Jaʿfarī Palace, which he in turn gave to his daughter.

Hāshimī (§§8.3.2, 8.3.4, 13.9, 14.2, 34.3, and n. 45) Member of the clan to which the Prophet Muḥammad belonged, so named for his great-grandfather. Also refers to anyone tracing descent from the Prophet Muḥammad, typically through his daughter Fāṭimah.

Ḥayāt Khātūn *(§32)* (d. 639/1241) Slave of Turkic origin belonging to the caliph al-Ẓāhir and mother of one of his sons. She was manumitted upon his death.

Haylānah *(§5)* (d. 173/789–90) Slave of Hārūn al-Rashīd, obtained from Yaḥyā ibn Khālid the Barmakid. When she died, the poet al-ʿAbbās ibn al-Aḥnaf composed an elegy to her. A neighborhood in west Baghdad is named for her. See Map 2.

al-Haytham ibn Bassām (§11) (fl. second/eighth c.) Son of Bassām ibn Ibrāhīm, a dependent of the Banū Layth, and husband of **Farīdah al-Amīniyyah** (§11).

Ibn Ḥamdūn, Abū ʿAbd Allāh (§§8.6, 19.2, 36) (fl. late third/ninth c.) Aḥmad ibn Ibrāhīm, a poet and a member of the Ḥamdūn family of caliphal court companions.

Ibn al-Muʿtazz (§§6.6, 13.7, 31) (d. 296/908) ʿAbbasid prince, son of the caliph al-Muʿtazz; very significant poet, litterateur, and literary theorist, and an expert on the lives of early Abbasid poets, especially the "moderns" (*muḥdathūn*). He was installed as caliph at the age of forty-nine, on 20 Rabiʿ al-Awwal, 296/17 December 908, and assassinated the same day.

Ibn Rāʾiq (§36) (d. 330/942) Abū Bakr Muḥammad, chief of police and chamberlain under the caliph al-Muqtadir, then governor of Basra and Wāsiṭ under the caliphs al-Qāhir and al-Rāḍī, respectively. He was killed by the Ḥamdānids, who saw him as a threat. The first person to hold the title *amīr al-umarāʾ* (commander-in-chief of the army) under the Abbasids, he ushered in a period of militarism and the political decline of the Abbasids.

Ibrāhīm ibn al-ʿAbbās (§8.3.4) (d. 243/857) al-Ṣūlī, well-known poet, state secretary, and governor, from a family of Turkic origin. He was the great-uncle of the scholar and court companion Abū Bakr al-Ṣūlī and a nephew of the poet al-ʿAbbās ibn al-Aḥnaf.

Ibrāhīm ibn al-Mahdī (§§3.9, 8.2, 16.2) (d. 224/839) Abbasid prince, son of al-Mahdī and Shiklah, a Daylamī concubine. A poet, composer, and musician, he was reluctantly drawn into political life by al-Maʾmūn's opponents and proclaimed counter-caliph. His partisans were soon defeated by al-Ḥasan ibn Sahl and he went into hiding. He was captured, briefly imprisoned, then pardoned by al-Maʾmūn.

Ibrāhīm ibn al-Mudabbir (§13.7) (d. 279/892–93) High official, courtier, and litterateur. A companion of the caliph al-Mutawakkil, he was removed by enemies at court and imprisoned by them and later again by rebels associated with the Zanj slave rebellion in southern Iraq. He escaped and was later briefly vizier to the caliph al-Muʿtamid. He was the author of prose works and poems, many of the latter addressed to **ʿArīb.**

Ibrāhīm ibn al-Walīd (§37.4) (r. 126/744) Thirteenth caliph of the Umayyad dynasty, who reigned for only a few months. Ibn al-Sāʿī inherits a common error by identifying Ibrāhīm as the son of the royal Shāh-i Āfrīd, granddaughter of Yazdagird III; his mother was in fact a slave by the name of Suʿār.

Ibrāhīm al-Muʾayyad (§12.1) (fl. third/ninth c.) Son of the caliph al-Mutawakkil and **Isḥāq al-Andalusiyyah** (§12), a slave of mixed parentage.

ʿInān (§3) (d. 226/840–41) Slave who belonged to a certain al-Nāṭifī. Poets, including such renowned ones as Abū Nuwās and Marwān ibn Abī Ḥafṣah, came to al-Nāṭifī's home to have ʿInān pronounce on their poetry.

ʿĪsā (ibn ʿAlī) (§1) (d. 164/780–81) Paternal uncle of the caliphs al-Saffāḥ and al-Manṣūr. His daughter **Ḥammādah** (§1) was married to al-Manṣūr. The ʿĪsā Palace and the ʿĪsā Quarter in West Baghdad were named for him.

Isḥāq al-Andalusiyyah (§12) (d. 270/883) Slave of mixed parentage, one of al-Mutawakkil's favorites, and the mother of his sons al-Muwaffaq and al-Muʾayyad. On her death, ʿAlī ibn Yaḥyā composed an elegy to console al-Muwaffaq.

Isḥāq ibn Ayyūb al-Ghālibī (§7.2) (d. 287/900) Official who later in life was in charge of security in Diyār Rabīʿah in northern Iraq.

Isḥāq al-Mawṣilī (§6.4) (d. 235/850) The greatest musician of his day, leader of the "classical school," a popular courtier, litterateur, and a source of much palace history. In addition to books on music, he also produced a list of the "Top Hundred Songs" for the caliph al-Wāthiq, a genre which Abū l-Faraj al-Iṣfahānī later developed on a much larger scale in his *Book of Songs*.

ʿIṣmah Khātūn (§§24, 26) (d. 536/1141–42) Daughter of Sultan Malik-Shāh and sister of Sultan Muḥammad. She was married to the caliph al-Mustaẓhir and bore him a son, Abū Isḥāq Ibrāhīm, who died young. When al-Mustaẓhir died she returned to her native Isfahan where she famously endowed a Ḥanafī law college.

Jaʿfar (§§24.1, 25.1, 25.2) (d. 486/1093) Prince Abū l-Faḍl, son of the caliph al-Muqtadī and **Māh-i Mulk** (§25), daughter of Sultan Malik-Shāh. He died at the age of five and was buried in the Ruṣāfah Cemetery.

Jaʿfar ibn Yaḥyā ibn Khālid the Barmakid (§§6.1–6.3, 8.8.1–8.8.4) (d. 187/803) Son of the mentor and vizier of Hārūn al-Rashīd. He was very close to Hārūn and was his chief aide until Hārūn imprisoned and executed him in obscure circumstances. The change in fortune and subsequent downfall of the Barmakid family is often attributed to Jaʿfar's supposed marriage to ʿAbbāsah, al-Rashīd's sister.

Jamāl al-Dīn Baklak al-Nāṣirī (§30.1) (d. 635/1237) Royal slave soldier and commander. He was married to Khatā Khātūn, who raised **Shāhān** (§30).

***Khallāfah** (§20)* (fl. late third/ninth c.) Dependent of the caliph al-Muʿtamid; she bore him a son. She had a learned slave of her own called Munyah the Scribe.

***Khamrah** (§23)* (d. 378/988) Mother of the caliph al-Muqtadir's son ʿĪsā, remembered for her piety and generosity.

Khatā Khātūn (§§30.1, 30.4.1, 30.4.2) (fl. seventh/thirteenth c.) Daughter of the commander Sunqur al-Nāṣirī the Tall and a Turkic slave by the name of Qaṭr al-Nadā; wife of the commander Jamāl al-Dīn Baklak al-Nāṣirī. She raised and educated **Shāhān** (§30), whom she presented to the caliph al-Mustanṣir. She resided in what was once the palace of **Banafshā** (§27).

***Khātūn** (§24 and §26)* See **ʿIṣmah Khātūn**.

***Khātūn** (§38)* (d. 487/1094) Wife of Sultan Malik-Shāh and mother of Maḥmūd and of **Māh-i Mulk** (§25). Her name was Terken (also written Turkān).

Khātūn al-Safariyyah *(§37)* (d. 466/1073–74) Concubine of Sultan Malik-Shāh and the mother of his sons, Muḥammad and Sanjar.

al-Khayzurān (§37.4) (d. 173/789) Slave of Yemeni origin who was freed and married to the caliph al-Mahdī. She was the mother of the caliphs Mūsā al-Hādī and Hārūn al-Rashīd and of a daughter, al-Banūqah.

Khumārawayh (§22) (r. 270–82/884–96) Second Tulunid ruler of Egypt and Syria, whose relations with the Abbasid regent al-Muwaffaq were strained. He offered his daughter **Qaṭr al-Nadā** (§22) to the caliph al-Muʿtaḍid's son ʿAlī, but al-Muʿtaḍid married her himself. Khumārawayh was a patron of scholarship and the arts.

Kisrā (§8.3.4, n. 45) Persian Khusraw, applied to monarchs of the royal family of the Sassanids, who ruled Persia before the Arab Muslim conquests.

***Māh-i Mulk** (§25)* (d. ca. 484/1091) Daughter of Sultan Malik-Shāh and Terken **Khātūn** (§38); wife of al-Muqtadī and mother of their son Jaʿfar, who died young. She is also referred to in sources as Muh Malak and Malik Khātūn.

***Maḥbūbah** (§15)* (fl. second half of the third/ninth c.) Slave of the caliph al-Mutawakkil, described as one of the foremost singers and poets of her generation. When al-Mutawakkil died she became the property of Waṣīf, whom she angered, whereupon Bughā asked for her and freed her.

al-Mahdī (§§4, 37.4) (r. 775–85) Third Abbasid caliph, the father of two future caliphs, al-Hādī and Hārūn al-Rashīd, whose mother was his wife and former slave al-Khayzurān; of Ibrāhīm ibn al-Mahdī, whose mother was his slave and wife Shiklah; and of ʿAbbāsah, who was married to Jaʿfar the Barmakid.

Maḥmūd (§§37.3, 38) The son of Sultan Malik-Shāh and Terken **Khātūn** (§38). When Malik-Shāh died, Maḥmūd was only four years old and was Sultan (r. 485–87/1092–94) under the regency of his mother. He and his mother were soon killed by other claimants.

Malik-Shāh (§§24, 25, 25.2, 37.1, 37.4, 38) (r. 465–85/1072–92) Saljūq Sultan, the son of Alp Arslān. During his reign the Saljūq empire reached its greatest extent. He is praised in the sources as a noble and generous ruler. His wife Terken **Khātūn** (§38) bore him **Māh-i Mulk** (§25), who married the caliph al-Muqtadī. His daughter **ʿIṣmah Khātūn** (§24, 26) was married to the caliph al-Mustaẓhir. His concubine **Khātūn al-Safariyyah** (§37) was the mother of his successors, Muḥammad and Sanjar.

al-Maʾmūn (ʿAbd Allāh) (§§6, 6.1, 6.6, 7, 8, 8.2–8.6, 8.8.2, 8.8.4, 8.9, 8.10, 9) (r. 197–218/813–33) Seventh Abbasid caliph, the oldest son of Hārūn al-Rashīd. His mother, Marājil, a Persian concubine from

Khurasan, died when he was young and he was raised by his stepmother Zubaydah, the mother of his brother and rival al-Amīn. He married **Būrān** (§8), the daughter of his general al-Ḥasan ibn Sahl. His slaves included **ʿArīb** (§6) and **Muʾnisah** (§9). He was both a soldier and an intellectual.

al-Manṣūr (§1) (r. 136–58/754–75) Second Abbasid caliph and brother of the first caliph, al-Saffāḥ; both were children of Sallāmah, a Berber slave from North Africa. He was the founder of the new Abbasid capital, Baghdad. He married **Ḥammādah** (§1), daughter of his uncle, ʿĪsā.

Marwān ibn Abī Ḥafṣah (§3.5) (d. ca. 181/797) Famous and accomplished oratorical poet from a family of poets originally from Yamāmah, as was **ʿInān** (§3), in whose entry he is mentioned.

Masʿūd (§§29, 39) (r. 529–47/1134–52) Saljūq sultan, grandson of Sultan Malik-Shāh.

Maẓlūmah (§4) Slave belonging to ʿAbbāsah; **Ghaḍīḍ** (§4) transmitted material from her.

Muʾayyad al-Dīn Abū Ṭālib Muḥammad ibn al-ʿAlqamī (§33) (d. 656/1258) Majordomo (*ustādh-dār*) of the Caliphal Palace at the time of the caliph al-Mustaʿṣim's accession, and subsequently his vizier.

Muḥammad (§§37.1, 37.4) (498–511/1105–18) Saljūq sultan, son of Sultan Malik-Shāh with **Khātūn al-Safariyyah** (§37).

Muḥammad ibn al-Faraj al-Rukhkhajī (§§13.2.2, 13.3) (fl. early third/ninth c.) The son of Faraj al-Rukhkhajī and the brother of ʿUmar al-Rukhkhajī, he purchased **Faḍl** the Poetess (§13) and offered her to al-Mutawakkil. Both Faraj and ʿUmar were prominent state secretaries under al-Maʾmūn and subsequent caliphs.

al-Muhtadī bi-llāh (§7.6) (r. 255–56/869–70) Fourteenth Abbasid caliph, son of al-Wāthiq and a Byzantine slave.

Mukhfarānah (§19.3) (fl. third/ninth c.) A *mukhannath* (cross-dresser or ladyboy) who owned Nabt (§19) before al-Muʿtamid purchased her.

Muʾnis ibn ʿImrān (§8.8.2) (fl. late second/early ninth c.) Companion of Jaʿfar the Barmakid.

***Muʾnisah** (§9)* (fl. early third/early ninth c.) Byzantine slave and one of al-Maʾmūn's favored concubines.

Munyah (al-Kātibah) (§20) (fl. late third/late ninth c.) Slave belonging to **Khallāfah** (§20), the concubine of al-Muʿtamid. Munyah was a scribe and has an entry in al-Khaṭīb al-Baghdādī's biographical work *History of Baghdad*.

al-Muqtadī bi-Amr Allāh (§§24.1, 25.1) (r. 467–78/1075–94) Twenty-seventh Abbasid caliph. He tried to reconcile opposing Sunni factions in Baghdad, expelled the vizieral Jahīr family, and attempted to control Saljūq influence on the caliphate. To that end he married **Māh-i Mulk** (§25), the daughter of Sultan Malik-Shāh.

al-Muqtadir bi-llāh (§§23, 23.1, 23.2, 24.1, 34) (r. 295–320/908–32, with two interruptions) Eighteenth Abbasid caliph, the son of al-Muʿtaḍid by a Byzantine slave named Shaghab. **Khamrah** (§23) bore him a son, ʿĪsā.

al-Mustaḍīʾ bi-Amr Allāh (§§27, 27.1, 27.2, 28, 30.4.1, 32) (r. 566–75/1170–80) Thirty-third Abbasid caliph, son of al-Mustanjid and Ghaḍḍah, an Armenian slave. He was very close to his Byzantine concubine **Banafshā** (§27). The manumitted slave **Sharaf Khātūn al-Turkiyyah** (§28) bore al-Mustaḍīʾ a son, Abū Manṣūr Hāshim.

al-Mustanṣir bi-llāh (§§30, 30.1, 30.4.1, 30.4.2) (r. 623–40/1226–42) Thirty-sixth Abbasid caliph, eldest son of the caliph al-Ẓāhir and a Turkic slave. He founded the Mustanṣiriyyah law college and patronized other buildings and institutions; the Mustanṣiriyyah survived the Mongol invasions and has recently been restored. Khatā Khātūn presented him with the Byzantine slave **Shāhān** (§30), whom she had raised and trained. A work on al-Mustanṣir's caliphate by Ibn al-Sāʿī does not survive.

al-Mustaʿṣim bi-llāh (§30.4.1) (r. 640–56/1242–58) Thirty-seventh and last Abbasid caliph.

al-Mustaẓhir bi-llāh (§§24.1, 24.2, 26) (r. 487–512/1094–1118) Twenty-eighth Abbasid caliph, whose rule coincided with the early Crusades. He played the role of peacemaker among the warring Saljūqs and married **ʿIṣmah Khātūn** (§24), the daughter of Sultan Malik-Shāh and sister of Sultan Muḥammad.

al-Muʿtaḍid (§§7.3, 7.4, 8.12, 21, 21.1, 22.1–22.3, 23) (r. 279–89/892–902) Sixteenth Abbasid caliph, son of the regent al-Muwaffaq and his slave **Ḍirār** (§21). Al-Muʿtaḍid married **Qaṭr al-Nadā** (§22), the daughter of Khumārawayh.

al-Muʿtamid (§§6.5, 19, 19.2, 19.4, 20) (r. 256–79/870–92) Fifteenth Abbasid caliph, son of al-Mutawakkil and his slave Fityān, but essentially a figurehead in the palatine city of Samarra, with real power being wielded by his brother al-Muwaffaq in Baghdad. His slave **Khallāfah** (§20) bore him one son.

al-Muʿtaṣim bi-llāh (§§10, 10.1, 10.2) (r. 218–27/833–42) Eighth Abbasid caliph, son of Hārūn al-Rashīd and the slave Māridah.

al-Mutawakkil ʿalā llāh (§§12.1, 13, 13.2.2, 13.3–13.5, 13.10, 14, 14.2, 15, 15.2–15.6, 16, 17, 18, 18.3, 21.1) (r. 232–47/847–61) Tenth Abbasid caliph, son of the caliph al-Muʿtaṣim and Shujāʿ, a Khwārazmī slave, he was a patron of poets and musicians. He replaced the old administrators and Turkic military governors with his favorites, such as al-Fatḥ ibn Khāqān, and with his own sons. One son, al-Muntaṣir, conspired with the disgruntled Turkic guard and assassinated him.

al-Muwaffaq bi-llāh (§§8.12, 12.1–12.3, 21.1) Regent and virtual caliph (256–78/870–92) during the caliphate of his brother al-Muʿtamid. He was the son of al-Mutawakkil and the slave **Isḥāq** (§12), who died in the year that he finally crushed the Zanj slave rebellion. The slave **Ḍirār** (§21) bore him the future caliph al-Muʿtaḍid.

Nabt (§19) (fl. third/ninth c.) A slave belonging to Mukhfarānah the Ladyboy, subsequently purchased by al-Muʿtamid. She was an accomplished poet and singer.

***Nāshib al-Mutawakkiliyyah** (§16)* Slave in the household of the caliph al-Mutawakkil, renowned for her singing.

al-Nāṣir li-Dīn Allāh (§§27.4, 29, 29.1, 29.2.2, 30.4.2) (r. 575–622/1180–1225) Thirty-fourth Abbasid caliph, son of the caliph al-Mustaḍīʾ and Zumurrud Khātūn, a Turkic slave. He is credited with restoring power and sovereignty to the caliphate and with reform. He was married to **Saljūqī Khātūn** (§29), the daughter of Qilij Arslān, and was very attached to her.

al-Nāṭifī (§§3, 3.2, 3.5–3.10) (fl. second/eighth c.) Abū Khālid al-Nāṭifī, **ʿInān**'s (§3) owner. His surname, in either the form al-Nāṭifī or al-Naṭṭāf, means seller of *nāṭif*, a sweet nut brittle.

Nuṣrah (§9) (fl. third/ninth c.) Eunuch of al-Ma'mūn's vizier, Aḥmad ibn Yūsuf.

Qabīḥah the Poetess (§15.4) (d. 254/868) Byzantine slave of the caliph al-Mutawakkil, renowned for her poetry and also her beauty, hence her apotropaic nickname Qabīḥah, "Ugly." Al-Mutawakkil's favorite concubine, she bore him two sons, the future caliph al-Muʿtazz and the Abbasid prince Ismāʿīl.

***Qabīḥah** (§34)* (fl. late third/ninth c.) Dependent in the household of al-ʿAbbās ibn al-Ḥasan, vizier to the caliph al-Muqtadir. She is the source for some of the verse of Abū Bakr al-Ḥasan ibn al-ʿAllāf.

***Qaṭr al-Nadā** (§22)* (d. 287/900) Daughter of Khumārawayh and wife of the caliph al-Muʿtaḍid.

Qilij Arslān ibn Masʿūd (§29) (r. 550–88/1156–92) Properly Kılıç Arslan, Saljūq sultan.

***Qurrat al-ʿAyn** (§10)* (fl. third/ninth c.) Slave and favorite of the caliph al-Muʿtaṣim.

al-Rabīʿ ibn Yūnus (§11) (fl. late second/eighth c.) Chamberlain under al-Mahdī's reign of the future caliph Harūn al-Rashīd.

Sabians (§7.2) The Sabians of Harran followed an old Semitic polytheistic religion, with strong Hellenistic influences. By claiming to be the monotheistic *Ṣābi'ūn* mentioned in the Qur'an, they avoided religious persecution.

Saʿīd ibn Ḥumayd (§§13.6, 13.7) (d. ca. 250/864) A member of a noble Persian family, he was an accomplished prose stylist and headed the chancery under the caliph al-Mustaʿīn. He and **Faḍl al-Shāʿirah** (§13.6) were lovers.

***Saljūqī Khātūn** (§29)* (d. 584/1188) Saljūq princess and beloved wife of the caliph al-Nāṣir li-Dīn Allāh, who died two years after their marriage. She was also known as al-Akhlāṭiyyah, i.e. of Akhlāṭ, a town at the northwest corner of Lake Van.

Sanjar (§§37.1, 37.4) Saljūq ruler (r. 490–511/1097–1118), then sultan (r. 511–52/1118–57), son of Sultan Malik-Shāh and his concubine **Khātūn al-Safariyyah** (§37).

Sarīrah (§36) (d. 348/959) Slave of Ibn Rā'iq whom he purchased from Ibn Ḥamdūn. When Ibn Rā'iq died, the Hamdanid Abū 'Abd Allāh al-Ḥusayn ibn Sa'īd married her.

Shāhān (§30) (d. 652/1254–55) Byzantine slave belonging to Khatā Khātūn, who trained her and later presented her to the caliph al-Mustanṣir. She enjoyed the caliph's highest favor, held her own court, and engaged in many acts of patronage and piety.

Shāh-i Āfrīd (§37.4) (fl. second/eighth c.) Granddaughter of Yazdagird III, wife of the Umayyad caliph al-Walīd and held by some to be the mother of his sons, Yazīd and Ibrāhīm, both of whom became caliphs.

Sharaf Khātūn al-Turkiyyah (§28) (d. 608/1211) Manumitted slave of the caliph al-Mustaḍī' and mother of their son, Abū Manṣūr, whom she outlived.

Shāriyah (§15.3) (fl. third/ninth c.) Singer from Basra who was bought and trained by Ibrāhīm ibn al-Mahdī and who then herself had many students. She was a proponent of Ibrāhīm's style, unlike '**Arīb** (§6), who favored the classical style of Isḥāq al-Mawṣilī.

al-Sindī ibn al-Ḥarashī (§11) (fl. late second/eighth to early third/ninth c.) Husband of **Farīdah al-Amīniyyah** (§11). Like his uncle 'Abd Allāh ibn Sa'īd the governor of Wāsiṭ, al-Sindī was a supporter of al-Amīn before joining al-Ma'mūn.

Sitt al-Nisā' (§35) (fl. fourth/tenth c.) Daughter of Ṭūlūn the Turk, and a wealthy and prodigal woman whose fortunes turned.

Sulaymān ibn 'Abd al-Malik (§37.4) (96–99/715–17) Seventh caliph of the Umayyad dynasty.

Sunqur al-Nāṣirī the Tall (§30.1) (fl. late sixth/twelfth to early seventh/thirteenth c.) Turkic royal slave soldier and commander. He was the father of Khatā Khātūn, the woman who raised and trained **Shāhān** (§30).

Ṭūlūn the Turk (§35) (fl. fourth/tenth c.) Father of **Sitt al-Nisā'** (§35).

ʿUmar ibn al-Faraj al-Rukhkhajī (§13.2.2) (fl. early third/ninth c.) The brother of Muḥammad, both of them sons of al-Faraj al-Rukhkhajī. ʿUmar and his father were prominent state secretaries under al-Maʾmūn. ʿUmar was one of the officials who purchased the land for the construction of the palatine city of Samarra.

Umayyads (§8.2) Dynasty of caliphs who ruled the Islamic empire, principally from their capital Damascus, from 41/661 to 132/750, when they were overthrown by the Abbasids.

al-Walīd ibn ʿAbd al-Malik (§37.4) (r. 86–96/705–15) Sixth caliph of the Umayyad dynasty.

Wallādah bint al-ʿAbbās (§37.4) (fl. first/seventh to second/eighth c.) Highborn woman of Arabia, from the Qays tribe. She bore the Umayyad caliph ʿAbd al-Malik two sons, al-Walīd and Sulaymān, both of whom became caliph.

Waṣīf (§§7.3, 7.4) (d. 288/901) Turkic eunuch and general belonging to Muḥammad Ibn Abī l-Sāj, an Eastern Iranian noble. He was captured by the caliph al-Muʿtaḍid.

Waṣīf (§15.6) (d. 253/867) Turkic eunuch and military slave of al-Muʿtaṣim, and a general in the Abbasid army. He served as chamberlain to the caliphs al-Muʿtaṣim, al-Wāthiq, and also al-Mutawakkil, whom he betrayed.

al-Wāthiq (§§6.7, 18.3) (r. 227–32/842–47) Ninth Abbasid caliph, son of al-Muʿtaṣim and a Byzantine slave, Qarāṭīs. Although **Farīdah** (§18) belonged to the singer ʿAmr ibn Bānah, she lived with al-Wāthiq, who kept her as a concubine and favorite. He was also infatuated with one of her slaves.

Yaḥyā ibn Khālid the Barmakid (§§5, 6.1, 6.3) (d. 190/805) The most powerful of the Barmakids, father of al-Faḍl ibn Yaḥyā and Jaʿfar ibn Yaḥyā and foster father, mentor, and tutor to the future caliph Hārūn al-Rashīd. He was briefly imprisoned under the caliph al-Hādī, but as soon as Hārūn al-Rashīd came to power he made him his vizier. Yaḥyā sponsored and patronized the translations of works from Sanskrit and Middle Persian into Arabic. Abān al-Lāhiqī's versifications were apparently done at his behest.

Yāsir (§9) (fl. third/ninth c.) Eunuch in al-Ma'mūn's service.

Yazīd ibn al-Walīd (§37.4) (r. 126/744) Twelfth caliph of the Umayyad dynasty. He overthrew his predecessor but ruled only six months.

al-Ẓāhir bi-Amr Allāh (§§32, 33) (r. 622–23/1225–26) Thirty-fifth Abbasid caliph, remembered as just and pious; he ruled only nine months.

Zubaydah (§8.2) (d. 216/831) Her real name was Amat al-ʿAzīz bint Jaʿfar. She was the granddaughter of the caliph al-Manṣūr (who nicknamed her "little butter-ball," *zubaydah*), wife of the caliph Hārūn al-Rashīd, and mother of the caliph al-Amīn. A religious woman, she performed many pious and charitable acts including the provisioning of pilgrims and the building of wells on the road to Mecca, which became known as Zubaydah's Road (*Darb Zubaydah*) (see Map 1). There was also a leasehold in north Baghdad named for her (see Map 2).

***Zubaydah** (§39)* (d. 532/1137–38) Zubaydah Khātūn, daughter of the Saljūq sultan Berkyaruq and wife of the Saljūq sultan Masʿūd, the grandson of Malik-Shāh.

Zumurrud Khātūn (n. 98) (d. 599/1203) Turkic slave and mother of the caliph al-Nāṣir li-Dīn Allāh. She was pious, charitable, and politically active. She strongly supported the Ḥanbalī legal school and endowed a law college for them. She had her own mausoleum built during her lifetime.

Unnamed Characters

Female servant (§6.7) belonging to Farīdah (the younger); the caliph al-Wāthiq was infatuated with her.

Grandmother of Būrān (§8.2).

Mother of Khātūn al-Safariyyah (§37.2).

Authorities Cited by Ibn al-Sāʿī

Note: All the individuals are from Baghdad or based there unless otherwise noted.

Authors of Written Works Cited by Ibn al-Sāʿī

Abū Bakr al-Ṣūlī (§§6.3, 8.1, 8.4, 11, 18.1) (d. 335/946) Muḥammad ibn Yaḥyā, a leading literary scholar, author, anthologist, chess master, and court companion of several caliphs. Al-Muqtadir appointed him tutor to his sons, including the future caliph al-Rāḍī. His surviving works provide a great deal of information about poetry and the court. Ibn al-Sāʿī cites him without specifying the work.

Abū l-Faraj al-Iṣfahānī (§§3.2, 3.5–3.9, 3.11, 6.4, 6.5, 7.1, 7.3, 7.4, 13.2.1, 13.3–13.7, 14.1, 14.2, 15.2–15.6, 18.2, 19.1, 19.3) (d. ca. 360/971) ʿAlī ibn al-Ḥusayn, important litterateur and anthologist whose works rely on his considerable knowledge of both poetry and music and on a wide network of literary and scholarly contacts. The monumental *Book of Songs* (*Kitāb al-Aghānī*), compiled over fifty years, and the slim *Slave Poetesses* (*al-Imāʾ al-shawāʿir*) are important sources for *Consorts of the Caliphs*, though Ibn al-Sāʿī mentions only the former by name.

Abū Ṭāhir al-Karkhī (§17) (d. 479/1086–87) Aḥmad ibn al-Ḥasan, scholar of Hadith known for his piety and author of a history that does not survive.

Hilāl ibn al-Muḥassin (§§8.7, 23.2) (d. 448/1056) State secretary, author, and historian belonging to a family of Sabian scholars and secretaries. His works include a general history, a history of viziers, and *Rules of the Abbasid Court* (*Rusūm dār al-khilāfah*), a volume on administrative matters and protocol at the Abbasid court. Ibn al-Sāʿī quotes his *History*.

Ibn Abī Ṭāhir (§§8.11, 13.3, 19.3, 21.2) (d. 280/893) Aḥmad, bookman, author, literary critic, and anthologist of Persian origin. His history of Baghdad (*Kitāb Baghdād*) was mined by al-Ṭabarī and other historians, including Ibn al-Sāʿī in *Consorts of the Caliphs*; only one volume is extant.

Ibn al-Jawzī (§29.3) (d. 597/1200) Abū l-Faraj ʿAbd al-Raḥmān ibn ʿAlī, major Ḥanbalī jurist, theologian, exegete, historian, preacher, and prolific author, particularly influential during the caliphate of al-Mustaḍīʾ (r. 566–74/1171–79), when he was in charge of several madrasahs during the period of the so-called "Sunni revival." His *Well-Ordered History* (*Muntaẓam*), an eighteen-volume history (in the published edition) covering the creation of Adam to 574/1178, survives, though Ibn al-Sāʿī quotes from a nonextant part.

Jaʿfar ibn Qudāmah (§§2.1.1, 3.8, 3.9, 6.6, 13.4, 13.6, 14.2, 15.3–15.5, 19.3) (d. 319/931) State secretary and litterateur who belonged to the circle of Ibn al-Muʿtazz. He is cited by Abū l-Faraj al-Iṣfahānī and described by al-Khaṭīb al-Baghdādī as a learned scholar and author. None of his works survive.

al-Jahshiyārī, Abū ʿAbd Allāh (§§8.3.3, 8.6) (d. 331/942) Muḥammad ibn ʿAbdūs, politically active scholar. He is known principally for his *Book of Viziers and State Secretaries* (*Kitāb al-Wuzarāʾ wa-l-kuttāb*), of which the one surviving volume shows him to be interested in intellectual and literary matters as well. Ibn al-Sāʿī cites a passage from a nonextant part.

al-Khaṭīb al-Baghdādī, Abū Bakr Aḥmad ibn Thābit (§20) (d. 463/1071) Hadith scholar, preacher, theologian, and author, notably of *The History of Baghdad* (*Tārīkh Baghdād*), an encyclopedia of several thousand scholars who lived in Baghdad or passed through it.

Muḥammad ibn Dāwūd ibn al-Jarrāḥ (§§13.2.2, 13.10) (d. 296/908) Important state secretary and administrator under several Abbasid caliphs; highly regarded litterateur and anthologist. His book on poets, *The Folio* (*al-Waraqah*), is extant, but a work on viziers exists only in fragments.

Muḥammad ibn ʿImrān al-Marzubānī (§7.5) (d. 384/994) Prolific author, biographer, and literary critic of Khurasani origin who held literary gatherings at his home in Baghdad. His book *Ashʿār al-nisāʾ* (*Poetry by Women*), survives in part, together with fragments of encyclopedias of poets and philologists.

al-Ṭabarī (§§4, 22.3) (d. 310/923) Abū Jaʿfar Muḥammad ibn Jarīr, polymath originally from Ṭabaristān. His vast Qur'an commentary and his monumental universal history, *The History of Prophets and Kings* (*Tārīkh al-rusul wa-l-mulūk*), are important in themselves as well as for the numerous lost works they cite.

Thābit ibn Sinān (§§7.2, 7.6, 36) (d. 365/975) Physician and scientist from a family of Sabian physicians originally from Harran, author of a highly regarded history of Baghdad covering the years 295–362/908–74. This *History* (*Tārīkh*) is a continuation of al-Ṭabarī's and was itself continued by Thābit's nephew, Hilāl ibn al-Muḥassin.

ʿUbayd Allāh son of Ibn Abī Ṭāhir (§§6.8, 8.7, 12.2) (d. 313/925) Author of a history of Baghdad, of which only extracts survive, a continuation of his father's *Book of Baghdad* (*Kitāb Baghdād*), a political, literary, and cultural history of the city. ʿUbayd Allāh was friendly with members of the Munajjim family of courtiers and litterateurs.

Ẓafar ibn al-Dāʿī al-ʿAlawī (§35.2) (fl. fifth/eleventh c.) Son of a prominent ʿAlawī missionary, and jurist who studied with al-Karājikī. He wrote a work titled *Amālī* (*Dictations*).

Individuals Appearing in Lines of Transmission

Note: An asterisk (*) before a name means that Ibn al-Sāʿī had direct personal contact with that individual.

al-ʿAbbās ibn Rustam. See Characters.

ʿAbd Allāh ibn Abī Saʿd (§3.7) (d. 274/887) Cites Masʿūd ibn ʿĪsā for an anecdote about **ʿInān** (§3).

ʿAbd Allāh ibn Abī Sahl (§8.4) (fl. third/ninth c.) Cited by ʿAwn ibn Muḥammad for an anecdote about **Būrān** (§8).

ʿAbd al-Raḥmān ibn Muḥammad al-Shaybānī (§1) (fl. sixth/twelfth c.) Transmitter, son of a well-known Hadith scholar.

**ʿAbd al-Raḥmān ibn Saʿd Allāh al-Daqīqī (§§6.4, 13.2.1, 14.2, 15.2, 19.3)* (d. 615/1218) Prominent Hadith scholar and one of Ibn al-Sāʿī's informants. He was known as al-Ṭaḥḥān as well as al-Daqīqī, both of which mean "Flour Seller" (which may have been his or his father's profession), and as al-Wāsiṭī, "of Wāsiṭ."

**Abd al-Wahhāb ibn ʿAlī (§§1, 6.2)* (d. 607/1210) Abū Aḥmad al-Amīn, highly respected and learned religious scholar, also known as Ibn Sukaynah. "Al-Amīn" means trustee (lit. trustworthy), i.e. an individual to whom judges would entrust the property of orphans and minors as well as property that was in dispute during legal proceedings.

ʿAbd al-Wāḥid ibn Muḥammad (§8.3.3) (fl. fourth/tenth c.) Informant of al-Jahshiyārī and Muḥammad ibn ʿImrān al-Marzubānī; he transmitted from Maymūn ibn Hārūn.

Ibn Ḥamdūn, (§§8.6, 19.2, 36) (fl. third/ninth c.) Abū ʿAbd Allāh, member of the Ḥamdūn family of caliphal court companions. See also Ibn Ḥamdūn in Characters.

Abū l-ʿAbbās al-Marwazī (§13.5) (fl. third/ninth c.) Cited by Muḥammad ibn Khalaf for an anecdote about **Faḍl al-Shāʿirah** (§13.5).

**Abū ʿAbd Allāh al-Baghdādī (§§16.2, 31.2, 34.2, 35.2)* (d. 643/1245) Muḥammad ibn Maḥmūd, historian, Hadith scholar, and director of the Muṣtansiriyyah Law College in Baghdad; also known as Ibn al-Najjār. His numerous works include a continuation of al-Khaṭīb al-Baghdādī's *History of Baghdad* (*Tārikh Baghdād*).

Abū ʿAbd Allāh al-Ḥanbalī (§35.2) (d. 610/1213–14) Ḥanbalī jurist in Isfahan, with whom Abū ʿAbd Allāh al-Baghdādī studied.

Abū ʿAbd Allāh Muḥammad ibn al-Muʿallā (§§34.1–34.3) (fl. late third/ninth c.) Author of several works, including one titled *Dictations* (*Amālī*). He was also known as al-Azdī ("of Azd") and al-Baṣrī ("of Basra").

Abū ʿAlī al-Azdī (§8.8.2) (fl. fourth/tenth) Cited by al-Māwardī for an anecdote about Jaʿfar the Barmakid (§8.8.2).

Abū ʿAlī al-Bardānī (§22.2) (d. 498/1105) Aḥmad ibn Muḥammad, leading Ḥanbalī Hadith scholar.

Abū ʿAlī al-Ḥusayn ibn Abī l-Qāsim al-Qāshānī (§31.2) (fl. fourth/tenth) Cites Ibn al-ʿAllāf al-Shīrāzī for an anecdote about **Dawlah** (§31).

Abū ʿAlī ibn Mahdī (§23.1) (fl. fourth/tenth c.) Transmitter of an anecdote reported by al-Muqtadir's grandson about **Khamrah** (§23).

Abū ʿAlī al-Kawkabī (§8.5) (d. 327/939) al-Ḥusayn ibn al-Qāsim, litterateur and transmitter who reported from Abū l-Faḍl al-Rabaʿī, Abū l-ʿAynāʾ and others.

Abū ʿAlī al-Naṭṭāḥah See Characters.

Abū ʿAlī al-Rāzī (§13.8) (fl. fourth/tenth c.) al-Ḥasan ibn al-Qāsim al-Naḥwī, grammarian and lexicographer who frequented the court of the vizier, litterateur, and patron al-Ṣāḥib ibn ʿAbbād.

Abū l-ʿAynāʾ See Characters.

Abū Bakr al-Ḥanbalī (§10.2) (d. 563/1168) Aḥmad ibn al-Muqarrab, cited by Abū Muḥammad al-Junābidhī for an anecdote about **Qurrat al-ʿAyn** (§10). He was one of the teachers of Abū l-Qāsim ʿAlī, the son of Ibn al-Jawzī.

Abū Bakr al-Ḥasan ibn al-ʿAllāf (§§34.1, 34.3) (d. 318/930) Poet and scholar of poetry. He was an intimate of the caliph Ibn al-Muʿtazz, to the extent that a poem lamenting the death of his cat was thought by many to be an elegy on the caliph.

Abū Bakr ibn al-ʿAllāf al-Shīrāzī (§31.2) (d. 377/987–88) Aḥmad ibn ʿAbd al-Raḥmān, highly regarded grammarian, Hadith scholar, poet, and scholar of poetry.

Abū Bakr Muḥammad ibn al-Qāsim al-Anbārī (§6.2) (d. 328/940) Accomplished philologist, author of linguistic treatises, and teacher, known as Ibn al-Anbārī. His transmissions are quoted by Abū l-Faraj al-Iṣfahānī in the *Book of Songs* (*Kitāb al-Aghānī*).

Abū Bakr al-Ṣūlī See Authors.

Abū l-Faḍl al-Rabaʿī (§8.5) (fl. third/ninth c.) Transmitter cited by Abū ʿAlī al-Kawkabī for an anecdote about **Būrān** (§8.5).

Abū l-Faḍl Zayd ibn ʿAlī al-Rāzī (§31.2) (fl. fourth/tenth c.) Judge cited by Abū Naṣr al-Shīrāzī for an anecdote about **Dawlah** (§31).

Abū l-Faraj al-Ḥarrānī (§23.1) (d. 476/1083) ʿAbd Allāh, cites Abū ʿAlī ibn Mahdī for an anecdote about **Khamrah** (§23).

Abū l-Faraj al-Muʿāfā ibn Zakariyyāʾ al-Jarīrī (§16.2) (d. 390/1000) Judge; highly regarded scholar of jurisprudence, grammar, and other disciplines; follower of al-Ṭabarī's Jarīrī school of legal thought; and prolific author. His surviving work, a literary anthology designed to cheer and uplift,

The Good and Sufficient Companion and Consoling Counsellor (*al-Jalīs al-ṣāliḥ al-kāfī wa-l-anīs al-nāṣiḥ al-shāfī*), draws on a wide circle of informants.

Abū Ghālib al-Karkhī (§10.2) (d. 525/1131) Aḥmad ibn ʿAbd al-Bāqī, cited by Abū Bakr al-Ḥanbalī for an anecdote about **Qurrat al-ʿAyn** (§10). His reputation as a reliable transmitter was questioned by some.

Abū Ghālib Yūsuf ibn Muḥammad (§22.2) (fl. fifth/eleventh c.) Brother of Abū ʿAlī al-Bardānī, who cites him for an anecdote about **Qaṭr al-Nadā** (§22).

Abū l-Ḥasan ibn al-Ṣalt (§6.4, 13.2.1, 14.2, 15.2, 19.3) (fl. fourth/tenth c.) Aḥmad ibn Muḥammad, transmitted material from Abū l-Faraj al-Iṣfahānī.

Abū l-Ḥasan al-Māwardī, ʿAlī (ibn Muḥammad) al-Baṣrī (§§8.8.2, 34.2, 34.3) (d. 450/1058) Renowned Shāfiʿī jurist who held high office under several caliphs and author of numerous important treatises on law, government, and philology.

Abū l-Ḥasan Muḥammad ibn al-Qāsim al-Fārisī (§35.2) (fl. fifth/eleventh c.) Cited by Ẓafar ibn al-Dāʿī al-ʿAlawī in the entry on **Sitt al-Nisāʾ** (§35).

Abū Hāshim (§6.2) (fl. fourth/tenth c.) Cites Maymūn ibn Hārūn for an anecdote about **ʿArīb** (§6).

Abū l-Maḥāsin al-Jawharī (§35.2) (fl. late fifth/twelfth c.) Cited by Abū ʿAbd Allāh al-Baghdādī for an anecdote about **Sitt al-Nisāʾ** (§35).

Abū Manṣūr al-ʿUkbarī (§§6.4, 13.2.1, 14.2, 15.2, 19.3) (fl. sixth/twelfth c.) Muḥammad ibn Muḥammad ibn Aḥmad, transmitter of hadiths and literary-historical material and member of a family of Hadith scholars.

Abū Muḥammad ʿAbd Allāh ibn (Aḥmad) al-Khashshāb (§34.3) (d. 567/1172) Wide-ranging scholar, chiefly remembered as a grammarian.

Abū Muḥammad al-Anbārī (§6.2; n. 24) (d. ca. 304/916) Al-Qāsim ibn Muḥammad, philologist, father of the equally prominent philologist Abū Bakr Muḥammad ibn al-Qāsim al-Anbārī.

Abū Muḥammad al-Ḥasan son of ʿĪsā (§23.1) See Characters.

Abū Muḥammad al-Junābidhī (§10.2) (d. 611/1214) ʿAbd al-ʿAzīz ibn Abī Naṣr, scholar, also known as Ibn al-Akhḍar, who counted among his students the scholar and manumitted slave Yāqūt, whose encyclopedic dictionary of literary geography and bio-bibliographical dictionary are indispensable sources for scholars.

Abū Naṣr ʿAbd al-Karīm ibn Muḥammad al-Shīrāzī (§31.2) (fl. fifth/eleventh c.) Cited by Abū l-Rajāʾ al-Kisāʾī for an anecdote about **Dawlah** (§31).

Abū Naṣr Maḥmūd ibn Faḍl al-Iṣfahānī (§34.2) (fl. sixth/twelfth c.) Cites Abū l-Qāsim al-Rabaʿī for an anecdote about **Qabīḥah** (§34).

Abū Naṣr al-Manṣūr ibn ʿAbd Allāh al-Iṣfahānī (§35.2) (fl. fifth/eleventh c.) Cited by Abū l-Ḥasan ibn Muḥammad ibn al-Qāsim al-Fārisī for an anecdote about **Sitt al-Nisāʾ** (§35).

**Abū l-Qāsim ʿAlī ibn ʿAbd al-Raḥmān (§8.8.2)* (d. 630/1233) Son of the prominent author, historian, preacher, and public figure Ibn al-Jawzī, and one of Ibn al-Sāʿī's informants.

**Abū l-Qāsim al-Azajī (§31.2)* (d. 593/1196–97) ʿAbd al-ʿAzīz ibn ʿAlī, one of Ibn al-Sāʿī's teachers. "Azajī" refers to the Azaj Gate (*Bāb al-Azaj*), where there were several law colleges and many gatherings of religious and legal scholars.

Abū l-Qāsim ibn al-Samarqandī (§§6.4, 13.2.1, 14.2, 15.2, 19.3) (d. 536/1142) Ismāʿīl ibn Aḥmad, preeminent Hadith scholar, originally from Damascus.

Abū l-Qāsim al-Rabaʿī, ʿAlī ibn Ḥusayn (§§8.8.2, 34.2) (d. 502/1109) Important transmitter who studied with the great scholars of his day and was the teacher of a great many others.

Abū l-Rajāʾ Aḥmad ibn Muḥammad al-Kisāʾī (§31.2) (fl. sixth/twelfth c.) Cited by Abū l-Qāsim al-Azajī for an anecdote about **Dawlah** (§31.2).

Abū Sahl Aḥmad ibn Muḥammad al-Qaṭṭān (§1) (d. 359/969–70) Learned scholar of Hadith; also transmitter of poetry and literary material, notably from the grammarians al-Mubarrad and Thaʿlab. "Al-Qaṭṭān," "the Cotton Carder," may refer to his profession or that of a forebear.

Abū l-Ṭayyib Muḥammad ibn Isḥāq ibn Yaḥyā al-Washshāʾ (§20) (d. 325/937) Grammarian and litterateur, tutor to the slave Munyah the Scribe. His *Brocade* (*Kitāb al-Muwashshā*) is a book of prose and poetry on refined behavior, elegant lifestyle, and chaste love.

Abū Yaʿlā Aḥmad ibn ʿAbd al-Wāḥid al-ʿAdl (§16.2) (d. 438/1047) Scholar of Hadith. The profession "al-ʿAdl" means "notary witness," i.e.

an individual on whom judges call to vouch for witnesses and for testimony.

Aḥmad ibn Abī Ṭāhir See Ibn Abī Ṭāhir in Authors above.

Aḥmad ibn ʿAlī al-Ḥāfiẓ (§22.2) (fl. fourth/tenth c.) Cites al-Ḥasan ibn Abī Bakr for an anecdote about **Ḥammādah** (§1). The title "al-Ḥāfiẓ," "master," implies that he had mastered one or more disciplines or subjects.

Aḥmad ibn al-Ḥasan ibn Sahl (§8.3.2) (fl. third/ninth c.) Son of al-Ḥasan ibn Sahl.

Aḥmad ibn Kāmil (§§10.1, 10.2, 16.1, 16.2) (d. 350/961) Abū Bakr ibn Khalaf ibn Shajarah, wide-ranging scholar and litterateur, appointed judge (*qāḍī*) in Kufa. He was a sometime follower of al-Ṭabarī's short-lived Jarīrī school of legal thought.

Aḥmad ibn Muʿāwiyah (§3.6) (fl. third/ninth c.) Transmitter of material to ʿUmar ibn Shabbah.

Aḥmad ibn Muḥammad al-Iṣfahānī (§16.2) (d. 576/1180) Prominent Hadith scholar, known as al-Silafī; originally from Isfahan, he settled in Egypt.

Aḥmad ibn al-Ṭayyib al-Sarakhsī (§19.2) (d. 286/899) Multifaceted scholar, accomplished and prolific author, and the most prominent disciple of the philosopher al-Kindī.

Aḥmad ibn ʿUbayd Allāh (ibn ʿAmmār) (§3.7) (d. 314/926) Friend of the poet Ibn al-Rūmī and of the scholar Muḥammad ibn Dāwūd, who employed him. He later worked for the vizier al-Qāsim ibn ʿUbayd Allāh.

ʿAlī ibn ʿAbd al-Jabbār (§35.2) (fl. fourth/tenth c.) Sufi. Cited by Abū Naṣr al-Manṣūr ibn ʿAbd Allāh al-Iṣfahānī regarding **Sitt al-Nisāʾ**, daughter of Ṭūlūn the Turk (§35).

ʿAlī ibn al-Jahm See Characters.

ʿAlī ibn Sahl ibn Abān See Characters.

ʿAlī ibn Shādhān (§6.7) (fl. early third/ninth c.) Abū l-Ḥasan, Baghdadi Hadith scholar, known also as al-Jawharī ("the jeweler") and al-Kātib ("the state secretary").

ʿAlī ibn Yaḥyā the Astromancer See Characters.

ʿArafah See Characters.

ʿArīb al-Maʾmūniyyah See Characters.

ʿAwn ibn Muḥammad (§8.4) (fl. third/ninth c.) Al-Kindī, important informant for Abū Bakr al-Ṣūlī.

Dhākir ibn Kāmil al-Ḥadhdhāʾ (§34.2) (d. 591/1195) Transmitter known for his quiet demeanor and considerable knowledge of traditions. The name al-Ḥadhdhāʾ suggests that he and/or his father was a shoemaker by profession.

al-Faḍl ibn al-ʿAbbās al-Hāshimī (§14.2) (fl. third/ninth c.) Cited by Yaḥyā, the son of ʿAlī ibn Yaḥyā the astromancer, for an anecdote about **Faḍl al-Shāʿirah** (§13).

Ḥammād ibn Isḥāq (§6.4) (fl. third/ninth c.) Courtier; son of the great musician Isḥāq al-Mawṣilī, whose books and songs he transmitted.

al-Ḥasan ibn Abī Bakr (§1) (fl. fourth/tenth c.) Transmitter cited by Aḥmad ibn ʿAlī for an anecdote about **Ḥammādah** (§1).

Hibat Allāh son of Ibrāhīm ibn al-Mahdī (§3.9) (d. 275/888) Son of the Abbasid prince Ibrāhīm ibn al-Mahdī.

Ibn Khurradādhbih (§15.3) (d. ca. 300/912) ʿUbayd Allāh ibn ʿAbd Allāh, geographer and musicologist whose *Book of Routes and Realms* (*Kitāb al-Masālik wa-l-mamālik*) is extant, as are fragments of a work on music and musical instruments (*Kitāb al-Lahw wa-l-malāhī*).

Ibn al-Muʿtazz See Characters.

Ibn Nāṣir (§6.2) (d. 550/1155) Muḥammad ibn Nāṣir ibn Muḥammad, learned and devout religious scholar.

Ibn al-Sāʿī (d. 674/1276) ʿAlī ibn Anjab al-Sāʿī, librarian at the Niẓāmiyyah and Muṣtansiriyyah Law Colleges in Baghdad, author of *Consorts of the Caliphs* and as many as a hundred other historical and literary-historical works, most of which survive only in quotations by later authors.

Ibrāhīm ibn al-ʿAbbās See Characters.

Ibrāhīm ibn al-Mahdī See Characters.

Ibrāhīm ibn Makhlad (§10.2) (d. 410/1020) Important transmitter, cited by ʿUbayd Allāh ibn Aḥmad al-Azharī for an anecdote about **Qurrat al-ʿAyn** (§10).

Ibrāhīm ibn al-Mudabbir See Characters.

Ibrāhīm ibn ʿUmar al-Barmakī (§6.2) (d. 445/1053) Hadith scholar. His surname comes from the village of al-Barmakiyyah in Iraq where his family lived.

ʿĪsā ibn ʿAbd al-ʿAzīz al-Lakhmī (§16.2) (d. 629/1231) Alexandrian informant of Abū ʿAbd Allāh al-Baghdādī. He was principally a scholar of Qur'an recitation.

Isḥāq al-Mawṣilī See Characters.

Jaḥẓah (§§3.9, 6.5) (d. 324/936) Aḥmad ibn Jaʿfar, descendant of the Barmakids. He was a musician, poet, and wit who kept company with Ibn al-Muʿtazz and Ibn Rā'iq. He wrote books on food and music and reportedly also wrote a work about the caliph al-Muʿtamid.

al-Jammāz (§§3.10, 8.8.2) (d. mid-third/mid-ninth c.) Abū ʿAbd Allāh Muḥammad ibn ʿAmr, satirical poet and friend of Abū Nuwās. He did not gain favor at court, though late in life he is said to have been summoned by al-Mutawakkil.

al-Jawharī (§3.6) (d. 323/935) Abū Bakr Aḥmad ibn ʿAbd al-ʿAzīz, Basran scholar and the most significant transmitter of material from ʿUmar ibn Shabbah. Abū l-Faraj al-Iṣfahānī and Muḥammad ibn ʿImrān al-Marzubānī transmitted from him.

Marwān ibn Abī Ḥafṣah See Characters.

Masʿūd ibn ʿĪsā (§3.7) (fl. late third/ninth c.) Cited by ʿAbd Allāh ibn Abī Saʿd for an anecdote about **ʿInān** (§3). He was also known as al-ʿAbdī.

Maymūn ibn Hārūn (§6.2) (d. 297/910) State secretary, litterateur, and one of Abū l-Faraj al-Iṣfahānī's informants for the *Book of Songs* (*Kitāb al-Aghānī*).

al-Mubārak ibn ʿAbd al-Jabbār al-Ṣayrafī (§§6.2, 16.2, 34.3) (d. 500/1107) Baghdadi scholar, known also as Ibn al-Ṭuyūrī.

**Muḥammad ibn ʿAbd al-Wāḥid al-Hāshimī (§34.3)* (d. 640/1242–43) Transmitter and Hadith scholar. He was a descendant of the caliph al-Mutawakkil; he was also known as Ibn Shufnayn.

Muḥammad ibn Khalaf ibn al-Marzubān (§§13.3–13.5) (d. 309/921) Philologist, transmitter, and translator of Persian works. His *Women and*

Love/Love Poetry (*al-Nisāʾ wa-l-ghazal*) is lost, but his *Superiority of Dogs to Many Who Wear Togs* (*Faḍl al-kilāb ʿalā kathīr mimman labisa al-thiyāb*) survives.

Muḥammad ibn Mazyad (§6.4) (d. 325/937) Author and transmitter of literary and historical material. He was the secretary of the famous grammarian and philologist al-Mubarrad. He was also known as Ibn Abī l-Azhar.

Mūsā ibn ʿAbd Allāh al-Tamīmī (§3.7) (fl. third/ninth c.) Cited by Masʿūd ibn ʿĪsā for an anecdote about **ʿInān** (§3).

al-Muẓaffar ibn Yaḥyā al-Sharābī (§7.5) (d. 348/959) Scholar and transmitter who counted among his students Muḥammad ibn ʿImrān al-Marzubānī. His grandfather "al-Sharābī" was cupbearer to the caliph al-Mutawakkil.

Saʿīd ibn Ḥumayd See Characters.

Thaʿlab (§1) (d. 291/904) Abū l-ʿAbbās Aḥmad ibn Yaḥyā, famous grammarian and philologist, court tutor, and author of numerous classic works, some of which are extant.

ʿUbayd Allāh ibn Aḥmad al-Azharī (§10.2) (d. 435/1043) Prolific transmitter.

ʿUbayd Allāh ibn al-Ḥusayn ibn ʿAbd Allāh al-Bazzāz al-Anbārī (§20) (fl. fourth/tenth c.) Authority who transmitted from the female slave, Munyah the Scribe.

ʿUbayd Allāh ibn Muḥammad al-ʿUkbarī (§6.2) (d. 387/997) Pious Hadith scholar, known also as Ibn Baṭṭah, whose Ḥanbalī activism led the caliph al-Rāḍī to condemn Ḥanbalism.

ʿUmar ibn Shabbah (§3.6) (d. 262/878) Authority on poets, literary material, and historical events; author of numerous books, including a lost *History of Medina* (*Tārīkh Madīnah*). Material transmitted by his students, notably al-Jawharī, is quoted extensively by Abū l-Faraj al-Iṣfahānī, al-Ṭabarī, al-Jahshiyārī and others.

Yaḥyā ibn ʿAlī (§§6.4, 14.2) (d. 300/912?) Abū Aḥmad Yaḥyā ibn ʿAlī ibn Yaḥyā, scion of a prominent family of courtiers, astromancers, caliphal companions, and men of learning active in the Abbasid court for two centuries, who bore the surname Ibn al-Munajjim after an ancestor who had served as a court astromancer. Yaḥyā was an accomplished poet, music theorist, philosophical theologian, and literary historian. He taught Abū Bakr al-Ṣūlī and is widely quoted by Abū l-Faraj al-Iṣfahānī.

Glossary of Places

Note: Paragraph references are provided only for those places specifically mentioned by Ibn al-Sāʿī.

Alexandria A city in northern Egypt, on the Mediterranean (see Map 1).

al-Anbār (§6.7) A town on the left bank of the Euphrates, about 60 kilometers east of Baghdad (see Map 1).

Armorers' Archway (§8.9) (*ʿAqd al-Zarrādīn*) An archway on the Road of the Two Archways, which ran north and parallel to the Muʿallā Canal in the area north of the caliphal palaces on the East Bank (see Map 4).

Artificer's Archway (§8.9) (*ʿAqd al-Muṣṭaniʿ*) An archway on the Road of the Two Archways, which ran north and parallel to the Muʿallā Canal in the area north of the caliphal palaces on the East Bank (see Map 4).

ʿAyn Zarbah Anatolian town (modern-day Misis/Yakapınar) near Adana, where Waṣīf the Eunuch was captured by al-Muʿtaḍid (see Map 1).

Azaj Gate A gateway in the later city of Baghdad that opened to the south. It was the site of numerous law colleges (see Map 4).

Azerbaijan (§8.9) (*Ādharbayjān*) A province of Iran, in the Caucasus, to the west and southwest of the Caspian Sea (see Map 4).

Baghdad The city founded by the caliph al-Manṣūr as the new Abbasid capital in 145/762. Construction was completed in 149/766. The fortified Round City he called Madīnat al-Salām, "City of Peace." The caliph al-Mustaʿṣim surrendered the city to the Mongols in 656/1258—during the lifetime of the author of *Consorts of the Caliphs* (see Maps 1–4).

Bakers' Market (§27.2) (*Sūq al-Khabbāzīn*) Located in the northern part of later Baghdad. It was near this market and the Iron Archway that Banafshā had a mosque built (see Map 4).

Balkh An important ancient city, the center of Buddhism and Zoroastrianism. The Barmakids were originally from Balkh (see Map 1).

Banafshā's Palace (§§27.2, 30.4.1) Palace built for Banafshā by the caliph al-Mustaḍī' in 569/1173–74. Shāhān also lived there (see Map 4).

Basra (§§13.2.1, 13.3) A port in southern Iraq and a major intellectual center (see Map 1).

Bīn Canal (§8.12) (*Nahr Bīn* or *Nahrabīn*) A transverse canal flowing west (from the Nahrawān Canal) to the Tigris. The construction and diversion of canals were a major factor in irrigation and in the supplying of water (see Maps 3, 4).

Bushrā Gate (§32) A gate on the western side of the Tāj Palace grounds (see Map 4).

Cairo (§16.2) City founded in Egypt by the Fatimids in 358/969 as their capital; subsequently one of the great metropolises and centers of commercial, cultural, and military activity (see Map 1).

Caliphal Palace (§§22.3, 24.1, 25.2, 27.2, 27.4) Magnificent palace begun by the caliph al-Muʿtaḍid in 289/902 and completed by his son al-Muktafī. It was located south of the former Ḥasanī Palace, along the Tigris. It was known as the Tāj Palace and also the Great Palace (see Maps 3, 4).

Diyār Rabīʿah Province of northern Iraq (see Map 1).

Euphrates (al-Furāt) (§31.2) One of the two great rivers of Iraq, flowing from the mountains of southeastern Turkey. It lies to the west of Baghdad (see Map 1).

Fam al-Ṣilḥ (§§6.6, 8.2, 8.10) The point where the Tigris and Sillas divide, north of Wāsiṭ; site of the estate of al-Ḥasan ibn Sahl (see Map 1).

Fārs (§8.3.1) The Arabic term for Persia (see Map 1).

Hamadhan (§8.9) (*Hamadhān*) A city in central Iran (see Map 1).

Ḥanbalī law college (§27.1) A madrasah founded by Banafshā on the site of her former palace, by the Azaj Gate (see Map 4).

Harran Town situated at the confluence of important caravan routes in northern Mesopotamia. Its intellectual and cultural importance was due in part to the school of Sabian translators based there (see Map 1).

Hārūnī Palace One of approximately twenty palaces built by al-Mutawakkil in Samarra, and the one where he spent most of his time.

Ḥasanī Palace (§8.8.1–8.12) A palace built by Jaʿfar the Barmakid on the East Bank, southeast of the Round City and at some remove from it. It was first known as the Jaʿfarī Palace and then, when it passed to al-Maʾmūn (who built an adjoining polo ground, racecourse, and game preserve), as the Maʾmūnī Palace. Al-Maʾmūn gave it to his father-in-law, al-Ḥasan ibn Sahl, and it became known as the Ḥasanī Palace. Its history is described in detail in *Consorts of the Caliphs* (see Maps 2, 3, 4).

Haylānah Quarter A neighborhood in western Baghdad named for Hārūn al-Rashīd's slave Haylānah (see Map 2).

Hijaz (§11) A region of Western Arabia, in which are located both Mecca and Medina (see Map 1).

Iron Archway (§27.2) (*ʿAqd al-Ḥadīd*) Located in the northern part of later Baghdad, near the Bakers' Market and the mosque built by Banafshā (see Map 4).

ʿĪsā Palace Palace on the west bank of the Tigris belonging to ʿĪsā ibn ʿAlī; because of the palace, the area was known as the ʿĪsā Quarter (see Maps 2, 3, 4).

Isfahan (§§24.1, 24.2, 25.1, 35.2) Major Iranian city, which flourished especially after the fifth/eleventh century (see Map 1).

Isḥāq al-Andalusiyyah's palace (§12.3) This was located in Ruṣāfah (see Map 2).

Jaʿfarī Palace See Ḥasanī Palace.

Karkh (§29.2.1) Name of area to the west and southwest of the Round City of Baghdad. Served by numerous canals, it was an important mercantile area. From the fourth/tenth century onward it had a significant Shiʿi population (see Maps 2, 3, 4).

Karkh landing (§29.2.1) A landing place for boats on the ʿĪsā Canal (see Map 4).

Khuld Palace (§8.10) (*Qaṣr al-Khuld, Qaṣr al-Khilāfah*) Caliphal palace built by al-Manṣūr to the northeast of the Round City, at a strategic point between the military areas of Ḥarbiyyah and Ruṣāfah. It was so named with reference to "The Eternal Garden" (*jannat al-khuld*; cf.

Q Furqān 25:15). Built 158/775, reportedly at the coolest spot in Baghdad (see Maps 2, 3, 4).

Khurasan (§§8.9, 8.10, 25.1) A region that today includes northeastern Iran, Afghanistan, and parts of central Asia. The Abbasids received strong support from Khurasan when they overthrew the Umayyads; it was in Khurasan (in Marw) that al-Ma'mūn was initially based (see Map 1).

Khurasan Road (§8.9) A main road running from the Bridge of Boats to the Khurasan Gate. It was so named because it extended in the direction of Khurasan to the northeast (see Maps 2, 3).

Lake Van A landlocked lake in present-day southeastern Turkey (see Map 1).

Ma'mūnī Palace See Ḥasanī Palace.

Ma'mūniyyah Quarter The name of the area that lay outside the caliphal palace walls on the East Bank. It took its name from the former presence there of al-Ma'mūn's palace and grounds. When the area was destroyed by flooding, it was rebuilt by al-Muqtadī (see Map 4.).

Mausoleum of the caliph al-Nāṣir's mother (§27.4) Shrine of Zumurrud Khātūn, located north of the mausoleum of Maʿrūf al-Karkhī (see Map 4).

Mausoleum of Maʿrūf al-Karkhī (§27.4) Shrine of a prominent early Sufi of Baghdad (d. 200/815–16), in Karkh in West Baghdad. It still stands (see Map 4).

Mausoleum of al-Mustaḍī' (§32) On the left bank of the Tigris, just north of the ʿĪsā Canal (see Map 4).

Mausoleum of Saljūqī Khātūn (§29.2.1–2) A mausoleum that Saljūqī Khātūn built for herself near the Karkh Landing and across the canal from the shrine of ʿAwn and Muʿīn (see Map 4).

Mecca (§§29.2.2, 37.1) Pilgrimage city in the Hijaz, on the eastern coast of the Arabian peninsula, connected to Baghdad by several pilgrim routes, including the famous Darb Zubaydah (see Map 1).

Muʿallā Canal (§8.9) An offshoot of the Mūsā Canal, serving the southern part of eastern Baghdad. It was named for a freedman of the caliph al-Mahdī who later commanded Hārūn al-Rashīd's forces (see Maps 2, 3, 4).

Mustanṣiriyyah law college A famous and magnificent madrasah (law college) where Ibn al-Sāʿī held a position as librarian. It was founded by the caliph al-Mustanṣir in 631/1234, north of the Tāj Palace. It survived the Mongol destruction of Baghdad, has recently been restored, and is now part of Al-Mustanṣiriyyah University (see Map 4).

Niẓāmiyyah law college A famous madrasah (law college) founded in 457/1065 by Alp Arslān's minister, Nizām al-Mulk, in the southern part of the city on the east bank of the Tigris. Ibn al-Sāʿī held a position there as librarian (see Map 4).

Pontoon bridge constructed by Banafshā (§§27.1, 27.2, 30.4.2) Located near Banafshā's Palace and connecting the East Bank to the Raqqah Gate (see Map 4).

Raqqah Gate (§27.2) The gate to the Raqqah Gardens on the west bank of the Tigris, opposite the Tāj Palace (see Map 4).

al-Ruṣāfah (§12.3) One of the three original northern sections of Baghdad, on the eastern bank, so named for a paved causeway across the swampy area of the Tigris. It was directly opposite the Khuld Palace and itself included a palace and estates granted to Abbasid families and military commanders. Construction began in 151/768 and was completed in 159/776. In later times, the tombs of the Abbasid caliphs were located here, along the riverbank (see Maps 2, 3).

Ruṣāfah Cemetery (§§9, 21.2, 23.2, 24.1, 25.2, 28, 33) Site of the tombs of many Abbasid caliphs (and others) (see Maps 2, 3).

Samarra (§§6.8, 15.3, 15.6) (*Sāmarrāʾ* or *Surra man raʾā*) Palatine town on the east bank of the Tigris, 125 kilometers north of Baghdad. The city was laid out by al-Muʿtaṣim in 221/836 and occupied by the Abbasid caliphs until 279/892. Its heyday was under al-Mutawakkil (see Map 1).

al-Shammāsiyyah (§9) One of the three original northern sections of Baghdad (the other two being al-Ruṣāfah and Mukharrim), to the east of al-Ruṣāfah. The Barmakids had their residences here (see Map 2).

Shrine of ʿAwn and Muʿīn (§29.2.1) The shrine of two descendants of ʿAlī ibn Abī Ṭālib, just south of the mausoleum of Maʿrūf al-Karkhī in Karkh (see Map 4).

Soghdia A region of Central Asia lying beyond the Oxus River (see Map 1).

Stone bridge (§27.1) A bridge constructed by Banafshā over the ʿĪsā Canal (see Map 3).

Sufi lodge (§29.2.2) Built by al-Nāṣir after 584/1188 next to the mausoleum of Saljūqī Khātūn, east of and across the canal from the shrine of ʿAwn and Muʿīn in Karkh (see Map 4).

Ṭabaristān A coastal plain region on the southern shore of the Caspian Sea (see Map 4).

Tāj Palace (§29.3) (*al-Tāj, Qaṣr al-Tāj*) See Caliphal Palace (and see Map 4).

Talas The Arabic name for Ṭarāz, a settlement (named for a river) where in 133/751 a battle was fought between the Chinese governor and an Arab commander. It is said that the Chinese prisoners taken captive here introduced papermaking to the Arabs (see Map 4).

Tigris (§§8.4, 8.9, 8.11, 27.1, 27.2, 29.2.2, 30.4.2) (*Dijlah*) A major river flowing south from southeastern Turkey through Iraq. The Round City of Baghdad was founded on its left bank and went on to occupy both banks, close to the ruins of the ancient Sassanian capital of Ctesiphon. This placement was important, as the Tigris, together with the systems of canals, watercourses, and waterwheels, supplied water to the caliphs and to the populace (see Maps 1–4).

Wāsiṭ (§8.4) An agricultural town and administrative center on the Tigris in central Iraq (see Map 1).

Willow Gate (§§27.2, 30.4.1) (*Bāb al-Gharabah*) One of the principal gates of the Tāj Palace grounds. It was so-called for a willow tree growing there (see Map 4).

al-Yamāmah (§§3.2, 13, 13.2.1) Part of the Najd region in the central Arabian peninsula (see Map 1).

Yemen The southwestern part of the Arabian peninsula (see Map 1).

Glossary of Realia

alchemy See *sickness* below.

ambergris (*ʿanbar*) (*§§8.2, 8.3.3*) A waxy substance produced by the digestive system of sperm whales which, when dried, acquires a pleasing fragrance. It was used both as an incense and on the person. See also *scented musk blend* below. On ambergris, see Kemp, *Floating Gold.*

astromancy (*§§6.2 [poem], 6.6 [poem]*) Attention to the stars was important to the Abbasids. Scholars practiced astrology as well as astronomy (al-Maʾmūn built an important observatory), and the two professions were combined in astromancy, from which several members of the Ibn al-Munajjim (astromancer) (§7.2 and passim) family of courtiers and caliphal companions and advisers took their name. See Pingree, "Astrology."

atonement for vows (*takfīr*) (*§2.1.1*) The conditions of atonement described here are a combination of those imposed for the breaking (*ḥinth*) of a major oath.

bestowal, bestrewal (*nithār*) (*§§8.3.3, 8.4*) From *nathara*, "to scatter," as it describes gifts scattered, strewn, or distributed either on a festive occasion such as the marriage described here or as largesse by superiors to inferiors, which is also relevant here. See *EI2*, "Nithār."

bridges (*jisr, qanṭarah*) (*§§27.1, 27.2, 30.4.2*) There were two main kinds of bridge in Baghdad: pontoon bridges, which were supported by boats floating side by side; and stone bridges.

candelabrum (*tawr*) (*§8.2*) Can be made of any metal. The one al-Maʾmūn gave Būrān was of solid gold.

ceremonial robe(s) (khilʿah, pl. khilaʿ) (§§6.5, 7.4, 8.3.1) An item of clothing (or several) conferred on someone to honor them. Often embroidered with bands of inscription bearing the giver's name and titles, called *ṭirāz* (see below). See *EI2*, "Khilʿa," and Sourdel, "Robes of Honor."

chess (shaṭranj) (§6.4) A game widely played by the elite in the Abbasid period. It is no surprise, therefore, that ʿArīb was accomplished at chess. The caliphal companion Abū Bakr al-Ṣūli, quoted in the paragraph before the one that mentions ʿArīb's prowess at chess (§6.3), is said to have been the greatest chess player who ever lived. "Al-Suli's Diamond" was a chess problem that was only solved a thousand years later, by Russian grand master Yuri Averbakh. See Shenk, *The Immortal Game*, 38, 239.

dampened canvas sheets (khaysh) (§3.8, §8.8.3) *Khaysh* is canvas, but the fact that the room is being cooled means that the sheets have been dampened and suspended and are being swung back and forth with a cord. This creates a draft of cool air.

dinar (dīnār) (§6.7 and passim) A gold coin originally weighing approximately 4.25 grams. It was the basis of the monetary system and a symbol of status and wealth. It was worth approximately ten times as much as a silver dirham in the second/eighth century and twenty-five times as much by the third/ninth century. (*Danānīr*, the plural of *dīnār*, was the name of a famous slave belonging to the Barmakids, unmentioned in *Consorts of the Caliphs*. On her, see Ziriklī, *Aʿlām*, 2:341.).

dirham (dirham) (§3.2 and passim) A silver coin, originally weighing just under 3 grams, in use up to the Mongol period. It was worth one tenth of a gold dinar in the second/eighth century but had fallen to one twenty-fifth by the third/ninth century and was sometimes much lower.

drinking, drinking companions See *wine* below.

Eggplant à la Būrān (§7.5, 8) Or eggplant Burānī (*bādhinjān Būrānī*). Būrānī is a generic term in Iranian cuisine used to describe dishes prepared with yogurt and cooked vegetables, served hot or cold. Būrān, the daughter of al-Ḥasan ibn Sahl and the wife of al-Maʾmūn, is credited with having created it, hence the name. See *EIran*, "Būrān" and "Būrānī," and Davidson, *The Oxford Companion to Food*, "buran."

Eid al-Fitr (ʿĪd al-Fiṭr) (§27.3) Festival of the Fast-Breaking, observed on the first of Shawwāl, the month following Ramaḍān. It is marked by a special congregational post-sunrise prayer, often held outdoors. The distribution of alms (called *zakāt al-fitr* or *ṣadaqat al-fiṭr*), usually one measure (*ṣāʿ*) of dates, is obligatory. See also *stipulated measure* below.

eunuch (khādim) (§§7.3, 9) These individuals were an important part of the military and of caliphal and domestic households; some achieved very high positions. On eunuchs, see Ayalon, *Eunuchs, Caliphs and Sultans.*

funeral procession (janāzah) (§1) The body, wrapped in a white cloth, is placed in a bier and then either carried, or passed along, on the shoulders of men. (For the funeral procession, see the poems at §§12.3 and 34.3.) Carrying the bier is regarded as virtuous but, especially in the case of a large funeral, some mourners wait at the gravesite for the arrival of the bier.

game preserve (ḥayr) (§8.9) An enclosed area, typically for the hunt.

given the oath of allegiance (būyiʿa) (§§2.1.1, 8.10, 18.3, 30.1) The caliphs were recognized when they were given the oath of allegiance (called the *bayʿah*) by senior officers of state, a mutually binding pledge. On this practice, see *EI3*, "Bayʿa."

gold-woven mat (ḥaṣīr min dhahab) (§8.4) A mat woven with gold thread, later found among the treasures of the Fatimids (see Ibn al-Zubayr, *Book of Gifts and Rarities*, 235); an object that traveled, as did the Umayyad surcoat (see below under *jewel-studded surcoat*).

grant of revenues (§8.3.1) During the period in question, this practice referred to the granting of the revenues from a given piece of land or (as here) administrative district, a donation known as *iqṭāʿ*. See *EI2*, "Iḳṭāʿ."

humors (§8.8.4) Ancient Greek medicine and its heirs held the view that the balance of four bodily fluids, the "humors," was responsible for one's health. See Isaacs, "Arabic Medical Literature."

hunting (§8.9) An important pastime of the caliphs. It is described in detail in a genre of poetry especially devoted to it (*ṭardiyyah*).

jewel-studded surcoat (al-badanah al-Umawiyyah) (§8.2) This was a short sleeveless surcoat (or waistcoat), studded with large pearls, rubies, and other gems. It belonged to ʿAbdah, who was the granddaughter of the first Umayyad caliph and the wife of the tenth caliph. It came into the possession of ʿAbd Allāh ibn ʿAlī (d. 147/764), the uncle of the Abbasid caliph al-Manṣūr, when he defeated the last Umayyad caliph, Marwān ibn Muḥammad. Hārūn al-Rashīd offered it to Zubaydah. See Ibn al-Zubayr, *Book of Gifts and Rarities*, 121–23 and 275 n. 6.

lute (al-ʿūd) (§§6.5, 15.6) Properly an oud. The Arabic *al-ʿūd* may be the origin of the European word "lute," but the Arabic instrument is not the ancestor of the European lute; rather, the two share a common ancestor. See Farmer, *History of Arabian Music*.

marriage-contract celebration (imlāk) (§8.3.3) From *amlaka*, "to enter into a marriage contract," this word refers specifically to the expenditures made on the occasion of the signing of the marriage contract.

mausoleum (turbah) (§§24.1, 27.4, 29.2.1, 29.2.2, 29.3, 32) The later entries in *Consorts of the Caliphs* bear witness to the increasing popularity of this type of funerary monument among the ruling classes of Baghdad. See *EI2*, "Turba."

paper (ruqʿah) (§§8.3.2, 8.3.3, 15.3) Paper is said to have entered Abbasid society after the capture of Chinese papermakers at the Battle of Talas in 133/751. Paper was certainly replacing papyrus and other writing materials by the late second/eighth century. And by the third/ninth century, books were proliferating thanks to the availability of paper. See Bloom, *Paper Before Print*.

polo (ṣawlajān) (§8.9) A game that originated in Persia, played by royals. As with so many Sassanian customs, it was adopted by the Abbasids.

racecourse (maydān) (§8.9) Horse racing was a regular pastime of the elite and the caliphs. When they built palaces, they built adjoining racecourses. The racecourse in Samarra has been excavated. See Northedge, "Racecourses at Sāmarrāʾ."

ribbon (ʿiṣābah) (§6.7) Wearing a ribbon on one's brow is a fashion attributed to ʿAbbāsah, the sister of Hārūn al-Rashīd. See Ibn al-Zubayr, *Book of Gifts and Rarities*, 307 n. 9, and Ziriklī, *Aʿlām*, 5:35.

rosary (subḥah) (§23.1) A string of beads, usually ninety-nine beads separated into sections of thirty-three, with one bead at the head of the rosary (called the *imām*).

scented musk blend (ghāliyah) (§15.3–15.4) An ointment made of a blend of musk, ambergris, and aloeswood. It was called *ghāliyah*, "expensive," because its principal ingredients were so costly. See Ibn al-Zubayr, *Book of Gifts and Rarities*, 260, n. 4.

sickness: "would sickness in the stone beget" (§3.7) This is an image from alchemy, which held that there were esoteric processes that could alter the nature of the elements. See Hill, "Literature of Arabic Alchemy."

stipulated measure (ṣāʿ) (§27.3) Before the end of the month-long Ramadan fast, every Muslim is required to distribute one *ṣāʿ* of grain or other food. The *ṣāʿ*, a cubic measurement, varied in quantity, but is somewhere between two cupped handfuls and five pints.

Sufi lodge (ribāṭ) (§29.2.2) A piously endowed residential establishment built for use by members of a Sufi order. Novices were trained there. See *EI2*, "Ribāṭ."

sweet nut brittle (nāṭif) (§3 n. 10) A sweet brittle or praline made with walnuts, pistachios, or almonds. For a medieval recipe see Ibn al-ʿAdīm, *al-Wuṣlah*, 2:637, cf. *Scents and Flavors*, 166 and 167; and for a modern one see Elias and Salloum, *The Sweets of Araby*.

ṭirāz (§27.2) Fabric with woven or embroidered inscriptions, a practice possibly started by the Umayyad caliph Hishām (r. 105–25/724–43). See *EI2*, "Ṭirāz," and Sergeant, *Islamic Textiles*, 7–15.

wedding present (niḥlah) (§8.2) A relatively rare word for "present."

wine (nabīdh, khamr); drinking; drinking companions (§§6.5, 6.5 [poem], 8.4 [poem], 8.8.2, 13.10 [poem], 15.3, 15.4 [poem], 15.5, 15.6, 18.2 [poem], 23 [Khamrah's name], 36) Wine (*khamr, nabīdh*) was made of grapes or dates and variously mixed with other ingredients. Drinking played a very important part in the life of many of the Abbasid elite, including the caliphs. The morning drink and the after-dinner drink were considered part of refined behavior, and caliphs chose their drinking companions from the social and cultural elite. Khamrah's name, meaning "Bouquet" (§23), is a reference to wine. See Kennedy, *Wine Song*.

Bibliography

Primary Sources

ʿAbbās ibn al-Aḥnaf, al-. *Dīwān*. Beirut: Dār Ṣādir li-l-Ṭibāʿah wa-l-Nashr, 1965.

[Ibn al-ʿAdīm, ʿUmar ibn Aḥmad.] *Al-Wuṣlah ilā l-ḥabīb fī waṣf al-ṭayyibāt wa-l-ṭīb*. Edited by Sulaymā Maḥjūb and Durriyyah al-Khaṭīb. 2 vols. Aleppo: Maʿhad al-Turāth al-ʿIlmī al-ʿArabī, Jāmiʿat Ḥalab, 1986.

———. *Scents and Flavors*. Edited and translated by Charles Perry. New York: New York University Press, 2017.

Ibn al-Jawzī, Abū l-Faraj ʿAbd al-Raḥmān ibn ʿAlī. *Al-Muntaẓam fī tārīkh al-mulūk wa-l-umam*. Edited by Muḥammad ʿAbd al-Qādir ʿAṭā and Muṣṭafā ʿAbd al-Qādir ʿAṭā, revised by Naʿīm Zarzūr. 19 vols in 18. Beirut: Dār al-Kutub al-ʿIlmiyyah, 1992–93.

Ibn al-Muʿtazz, ʿAbd Allāh. *Dīwān Shiʿr Ibn al-Muʿtazz, ṣanʿat Abī Bakr Muḥammad ibn Yaḥyā al-Ṣūlī*. Edited by Yūnus Aḥmad al-Sāmarrāʾī. 3 vols. Beirut: ʿĀlam al-Kutub li-l-Ṭibāʿah wa-l-Nashr wa-l-Tawzīʿ, 1997.

Ibn al-Sāʿī, ʿAlī ibn Anjab. *Al-Jāmiʿ al-mukhtaṣar fī ʿunwān al-tawārīkh wa-ʿuyūn al-siyar*. Edited by Muṣṭafā Jawād. Baghdad: al-Maṭbaʿah al-Suryāniyyah al-Kāthūlīkiyyah, 1353/1934.

———. *Al-Jāmiʿ al-mukhtaṣar fī ʿunwān al-tawārīkh wa-ʿuyūn al-siyar* . Edited by ʿĀrif Aḥmad ʿAbd al-Ghanī and Khālid Aḥmad al-Mullā al-Suwaydī. Damascus: Dār Kinān li-l-Ṭibāʿah wa-l-Nashr wa-l-Tawzīʿ, 2011.

———. *Al-Maqābir al-mashhūrah wa-l-mashāhid al-mazūrah.* No ed. Amman: Dār al-Fārūq, 2014.

———. *Mukhtaṣar akhbār al-khulafāʾ.* Būlāq: al-Maṭbaʿah al-Amīriyyah, 1309/1891.

———. *Nisāʾ al-khulafāʾ al-musammā Jihāt al-aʾimmah al-khulafāʾ min al-ḥarāʾir wa-l-imāʾ.* Edited by Muṣṭafā Jawād. Cairo: Dār al-Maʿārif, 1968.

——— [Tāj al-Dīn Abī Ṭālib]. *Nisāʾ al-khulafāʾ al-musammā Jihāt al-aʾimmah al-khulafāʾ min al-ḥarāʾir wa-l-imāʾ.* Edited by Muṣṭafā Jawād. Baghdad and Beirut: Manshūrāt al-Jamal, 2011.

Ibn al-Zubayr, Aḥmad ibn al-Rashīd. *Book of Gifts and Rarities = Kitāb al-Hadāyā wa al-tuḥaf: Selections Compiled in the Fifteenth Century from an Eleventh-Century Manuscript on Gifts and Treasures.* Translated by Ghāda al-Ḥijjawī al-Qaddūmī. Cambridge, MA: distributed for the Center of Middle Eastern Studies of Harvard University by Harvard University Press, 1996.

Ibn Wāṣil al-Ḥamawī. *Ishfāʾ al-qulūb bi-akhbār Banī Ayyūb/Tārīkh al-wāṣilīn fī akhbār al-khulafāʾ wa l-mulūk wa-l-salāṭīn.* Paris, Bibliothèque nationale, MS ar. 1702.

Iṣbahānī, Abū l-Faraj al-. *See* Iṣfahānī, Abū l-Faraj al-.

Iṣfahānī, Abū l-Faraj al-. *Al-Imāʾ al-shawāʿir.* Edited by Jalīl al-ʿAṭiyyah. Beirut: Dār al-Niḍāl, 1983.

———. *Al-Imāʾ al-shawāʿir.* Edited by Nūrī Ḥammūdī al-Qaysī and Yūnus Aḥmad al-Sāmarrāʾī. Beirut: ʿĀlam al-Kutub; Maktabat al-Nahḍah al-ʿArabiyyah, 1984.

———. *Kitāb al-Aghānī.* 20 vols in 10. Būlāq: al-Maṭbaʿah al-Amīriyyah, 1285/1868.

———. *Riyy al-ẓamā fī-man qāla al-shiʿr fī l-imā* [= *Al-Imāʾ al-shawāʿir*]. Edited by Laylā Ḥuramiyyah al-Ṭabbūbī. Beirut: Muʾassasat al-Intishār al-ʿArabī, 2010.

Jāḥiẓ, Abū ʿUthmān ʿAmr ibn Baḥr al-. *Risālat al-Qiyān/The Epistle on Singing-Girls of Jāḥiẓ.* Edited and translated by A. F. L. Beeston. Warminster: Aris and Phillips Ltd., 1980.

Jahshiyārī, Muḥammad ibn ʿAbdūs al-. *Kitāb al-Wuzarāʾ wa-l-kuttāb.* Edited by Ibrāhīm Ṣāliḥ. Abu Dhabi: Hayʾat Abū Ẓabī li-l-Thaqāfah wa-l-Turāth, 2009.

Jarīr ibn ʿAṭiyyah. *Dīwān.* Edited by Nuʿmān Muḥammad Amīn Ṭāhā. Cairo: Dār al-Maʿārif, 1969.

Khaṭīb al-Baghdādī, Abū Bakr Aḥmad ibn ʿAlī al-. *Tārīkh Baghdād aw Madīnat al-salām.* 14 vols. Beirut: Dār al-Kitāb al-ʿArabī, 1966.

Qifṭī, ʿAlī ibn Yūsuf al-. *Ibn al-Qifṭī's Tārīḫ al-ḥukamāʾ.* Edited by Julius Lippert. Leipzig: Dieterich'sche Verlagsbuchhandlung, 1903.

Ṭabarī, Abū Jaʿfar Muḥammad ibn Jarīr al-. *The ʿAbbāsid Caliphate in Equilibrium.* Translated and annotated by C. E. Bosworth. Albany, NY: State University of New York Press, 1989.

———. *Return of the Caliphate to Baghdad.* Translated and annotated by Franz Rosenthal. Albany, NY: State University of New York Press, 1985.

———. *Tārīkh al-rusul wa-l-mulūk.* Edited by M. J. de Goeje et al. Series I–III. Leiden: E. J. Brill, 1879–1901.

Washshāʾ, Muḥammad ibn Isḥāq al-. *Das Buch des buntbestickten Kleids.* Translated by Dieter Bellmann. Bremen: Schünemann, 1984.

———. *Kitāb al-Muwashshā.* Edited by Rudolph E. Brünnow. Leiden: E. J. Brill, 1886.

———. *El libro del brocado.* Translated by Teresa Garulo. Madrid: Alfaguara, 1990.

———. *Le livre de brocart, ou la société raffinée de Bagdad au Xe siècle.* Translated by Siham Bouhlal. Paris: Gallimard, 2004.

———. *Al-Ẓarf wa-l-ẓurafāʾ* [= *Kitāb al-Muwashshā*]. Edited by Fahmī Saʿd. Beirut: ʿĀlam al-Kutub, 1985.

Yāqūt ibn ʿAbd Allāh al-Ḥamawī. *Jacut's geographisches Wörterbuch* [= *Muʿjam al-buldān*]. Edited by Ferdinand Wüstenfeld. 6 vols. Leipzig: in Commission bei F. A. Brockhaus, 1866–73.

Secondary Sources

Ahola, Judith, and Letizia Osti. "Baghdad at the time of al-Muqtadir." In Maaike van Berkel et al. *Crisis and Continuity at the Abbasid Court: Formal and Informal Politics in the Caliphate of al-Muqtadir (295–320/908–932)*, 221–38. Leiden: Brill, 2013.

Al-Heitty, Abdul-Kareem. *See* Heitty, Abdul-Kareem, Al-.

Ali, Kecia. *Marriage and Slavery in Early Islam*. Cambridge, MA: Harvard University Press, 2010.

Ardener, Edwin. "Belief and the Problem of Women" and "The Problem Revisited." In *Perceiving Women*, edited by Shirley Ardener, 1–27. London: Malaby Press, 1975.

Ayalon, David. *Eunuchs, Caliphs and Sultans: A Study in Power Relationships*. Jerusalem: Magnes Press, The Hebrew University, 1999.

Bloom, Jonathan. *Paper before Print: The History and Impact of Paper in the Islamic World*. New Haven: Yale University Press, 2001.

Bray, Julia. "A Caliph and His Public Relations." In *New Perspectives on Arabian Nights: Ideological Variations and Narrative Horizons*, edited by Wen-Chin Ouyang and Geert Jan van Gelder, 27–38. London: Routledge, 2005.

Davidson, Alan. *The Oxford Companion to Food*. 2nd ed. Oxford: Oxford University Press, 2006.

Diem, Werner, and Marco Schöller. *The Living and the Dead in Islam. Studies in Arabic Epitaphs*. 3 vols. Wiesbaden: Harrassowitz Verlag, 2004.

Elias, Leila Salloum, and Muna Salloum. *The Sweets of Araby*. Woodstock, VT: Countryman Press, 2011.

EI2. See Encyclopaedia of Islam, Second Edition.

EI3. See Encyclopaedia of Islam, Three.

EIran. See Encyclopaedia Iranica.

Encyclopaedia Iranica, online edition, available at www.iranicaonline.org.

Encyclopaedia of Islam, Second Edition, edited by H. A. R. Gibb et al. 13 vols. Leiden: E. J. Brill, 1960–2009.

Encyclopaedia of Islam, Three, edited by Marc Gaborieau et al. Leiden: Brill, 2007–.

Farmer, Henry George. *A History of Arabian Music to the XIIIth Century.* London: Luzac & Co., 1994. First published 1929.

Hartmann, Angelika. "al-Nāṣir li-Dīn Allāh." In *Encyclopaedia of Islam, Second Edition*, vol. 7, edited by C. E. Bosworth et al., 996–1003. Leiden: E. J. Brill, 1992.

Heitty, Abdul-Kareem, Al-. *The Role of the Poetess at the ʿAbbāsid Court (132–247 A.H./750–861 A.D.): A Critical Study of the Contribution to Literature of Free Women and Slave-Girls under the Early Abbasid Caliphate, Their Biographies and Surviving Works.* Beirut: Al-Rayan, 2005.

Hill, Donald R. "The Literature of Arabic Alchemy." In *Religion, Learning and Science in the ʿAbbasid Period*, edited by M. J. L. Young et al., 328–41. Cambridge: Cambridge University Press, 1990.

Hillenbrand, Carole. "al-Mustanṣir (I)." In *Encyclopaedia of Islam, Second Edition*, vol. 7, edited by C. E. Bosworth et al., 727–29. Leiden: E. J. Brill, 1992.

Imhof, Agnes. "Traditio vel Aemulatio? The Singing Contest of Sāmarrā, Expression of a Medieval Culture of Competition." *Der Islam*, 90, no. 1 (2013): 1–20.

Isaacs, Haskell D. "Arabic Medical Literature." In *Religion, Learning and Science in the ʿAbbasid Period*, edited by M. J. L. Young et al., 342–63. Cambridge: Cambridge University Press, 1990.

Jawād, Muṣṭafā. "Introduction." *See* Ibn al-Sāʿī, *Nisāʾ al-khulafāʾ* under Primary Sources.

Jawād, Muṣtafā, and Aḥmad Sūsah. *Dalīl kharīṭat Baghdād al-mufaṣṣal fī khiṭaṭ Baghdād qadīman wa-ḥadīthan.* Baghdad: al-Majmaʿ al-ʿIlmī al-ʿIrāqī, 1958.

Kaḥḥālah, ʿUmar Riḍā. *Aʿlām al-nisāʾ fī ʿālamay al-ʿArab wa-l-Islām.* 5 vols. Revised and expanded edition. Beirut: Muʾassasat al-Risālah, 1977.

Kemp, Christopher. *Floating Gold: A Natural (and Unnatural) History of Ambergris.* Chicago: University of Chicago Press, 2012.

Kennedy, Hugh. *The Prophet and the Age of the Caliphates: the Islamic Near East from the Sixth to the Eleventh Century*, 2nd ed. Harlow, England; New York: Pearson/Longman, 2004.

Kennedy, Philip. *The Wine Song in Classical Arabic Poetry: Abū Nuwās and the Literary Tradition.* Oxford: Clarendon Press; New York: Oxford University Press, 1997.

Kilpatrick, Hilary. *Making the Great Book of Songs: Compilation and the Author's Craft in Abū l-Faraj al-Iṣbahānī's Kitāb al-Aghānī.* London: RoutledgeCurzon, 2003.

Lassner, Jacob. *The Topography of Baghdad in the Early Middle Ages.* Detroit: Wayne State University Press, 1970.

Le Strange, Guy. *Baghdad during the Abbasid Caliphate: From Contemporary Arabic and Persian Sources.* Westport, CT: Greenwood Press, 1983. First published 1900.

Lindsay, J. E. "Ibn al-Sāʿī." In *Encyclopedia of Arabic Literature,* vol. 1, edited by Julie Scott Meisami and Paul Starkey, 367–68. London: Routledge, 1998.

Makdisi, George. "The Topography of Eleventh-Century Baġdād: Materials and Notes (I)." *Arabica,* 6, no. 2 (May 1959): 178–97.

———. "The Topography of Eleventh-Century Baġdād: Materials and Notes (II)." *Arabica,* 6, no. 3 (September 1959): 281–309.

Northedge, Alastair. "The Racecourses at Sāmarrāʾ." *Bulletin of the School of Oriental and African Studies,* 53, no. 1 (1990): 31–56.

Pingree, David. "Astrology." In *Religion, Learning and Science in the ʿAbbasid Period,* edited by M. J. L. Young et al., 290–300. Cambridge: Cambridge University Press, 1990.

Reynolds, Dwight F., ed. *Interpreting the Self: Autobiography in the Arabic Literary Tradition.* Berkeley: University of California Press, 2001.

Robinson, Chase F. *Islamic Historiography.* Cambridge: Cambridge University Press, 2003.

Rosenthal, Franz. "Ibn al-Sāʿī." In *Encyclopaedia of Islam, Second Edition,* vol. 3, edited by Bernard Lewis et al, 925–26. Leiden: E. J. Brill, 1971.

Rowson, Everett. "Gender Irregularity As Entertainment: Institutionalized Transvestism at the Caliphal Court in Medieval Baghdad." In *Gender and Difference in the Middle Ages,* edited by Sharon Farmer and Carol Braun Pasternack, 45–72. Minneapolis: University of Minnesota Press, 2003.

Seidensticker, Tilman. "Ibn al-Jawzī." In *Encyclopedia of Arabic Literature*, vol. 1, edited by Julie Meisami and Paul Starkey, 338–39. London: Routledge, 1998.

Sergeant, R. B. *Islamic Textiles*. Beirut: Librairie du Liban, 1972.

Shenk, David. *The Immortal Game: A History of Chess*. New York: Doubleday, 2006.

Sourdel, Dominique. "Robes of Honor in ʿAbbasid Baghdad during the Eighth to Eleventh Centuries." In *Robes of Honor: The Medieval World of Investiture*, 137–45, edited by Stewart Gordon. New York: Palgrave, 2001.

Stigelbauer, Michael. *Die Sängerinnen am Abbasidenhof um die Zeit des Kalifen Al-Mutawakkil. Nach dem Kitāb al-Aġānī des Abu-l-Faraǧ al-Iṣbahānī und anderen Quellen dargestellt*. Vienna: Verband der Wissenschaftlichen Gesellschaften Österreichs, 1975.

Ziriklī, Khayr al-Dīn al-. *Al-Aʿlām*, 10th edition. 8 vols. Beirut: Dār al-ʿIlm li-l-Malāyīn, 1990.

Further Reading

The Abbasids—Political History

El-Hibri, Tayeb. *Reinterpreting Islamic Historiography: Hārūn al-Rashīd and the Narrative of the ʿAbbāsid Caliphate.* Cambridge: Cambridge University Press, 1999.

Hanne, Eric J. *Putting the Caliph in His Place: Power, Authority and the Late Abbasid Caliphate.* Madison, NJ: Fairleigh Dickinson University Press, 2007.

Kennedy, Hugh. *The Early Abbasid Caliphate: A Political History.* London: Croom Helm; Totowa, NJ: Barnes & Noble, 1981.

The New Cambridge History of Islam. Vol. 1: The Formation of the Islamic World, Sixth to Eleventh Centuries, edited by Chase Robinson. *Vol. 2: The Eastern Islamic World, Eleventh to Eighteenth Centuries,* edited by David O. Morgan and Anthony Reid. Cambridge: Cambridge University Press, 2010.

The Abbasids—Cultural History

Ahsan, M. M. *Social Life Under the Abbasids 170–289 AH, 786–902 A.D.* London: Longman, 1979. Reprint: Atlanta: Lockwood Press, 2017.

Bennison, Amira. *The Great Caliphs: The Golden Age of the ʿAbbasid Empire.* London: I. B. Tauris, 2009; New Haven: Yale University Press, 2009.

Journal of ʿAbbāsid Studies. <booksandjournals.brillonline.com/content/journals/22142371>.

Mez, Adam. *The Renaissance of Islam.* Translated by Salahuddin Khuda Bukhsh and D. S. Margoliouth. London: Luzac & Co., 1937.

Toorawa, Shawkat M. *Ibn Abī Ṭāhir Ṭayfūr and Arabic Writerly Culture: A Ninth-Century Bookman in Baghdad.* London: RoutledgeCurzon, 2004.

Baghdad

Antrim, Zayde. "Connectivity and Creativity: Representations of Baghdad's Centrality, 3rd/9th to 5th/11th Centuries." In *İslam Medeniyetinde Bağdat (Medînetü's-Selâm) Uluslararası Sempozyum/ International Symposium on Baghdad (Madinat al-Salam) in the Islamic Civilization*, edited by İsmail Safa Üstün, 55–74. Üsküdar, Istanbul: Marmara Üniversitesi, İlâhiyat Fakültesi, İslâm Tarihi ve Sanatları Bölümü, 2011.

Kennedy, Hugh. *The Court of the Caliphs: The Rise and Fall of Islam's Greatest Dynasty.* London: Weidenfeld & Nicolson, 2004 = *When Baghdad Ruled the Muslim World: The Rise and Fall of Islam's Greatest Dynasty.* Cambridge, MA: Da Capo Press, 2005.

Lassner, Jacob. *The Shaping of ʿAbbāsid Rule.* Princeton: Princeton University Press, 1980.

Court

Berkel, Maaike van. "The Vizier and the Harem Stewardess: Mediation in a Discharge Case at the Court of the Caliph al-Muqtadir." In *ʿAbbāsid Studies II: Occasional Papers of the School of ʿAbbasid Studies Leuven, 28 June–1 July, 2004*, edited by John Nawas, 303–18. Leuven: Peeters, 2010.

Berkel, Maaike van, Nadia El Cheikh, Hugh Kennedy, and Letizia Osti. *Crisis and Continuity at the Abbasid Court: Formal and Informal Politics in the Caliphate of al-Muqtadir (295–320/908–932).* Leiden: Brill, 2013.

Hilāl al-Ṣābi. *Rusūm dār al-khilāfah*. Edited by Mikhā'īl 'Awwād. Baghdad: Maṭba'at al-'Ānī, 1964. English translation: *The Rules and Regulations of the 'Abbāsid Court*. Translated by Elie Salem. Beirut: American University of Beirut, 1977.

Meisami, Julie S. "Mas'ūdī on Love and the Fall of the Barmakids." *Journal of the Royal Asiatic Society* (1989): 252–77.

Learning

Ephrat, Daphna. *A Learned Society in a Period Of Transition: The Sunni 'Ulama' of Eleventh-Century Baghdad*. Albany, NY: State University of New York Press, 2000.

Lowry, Joseph, Devin Stewart, and Shawkat M. Toorawa, ed. *Law and Education in Medieval Islam*. Cambridge: E. J. W. Gibb Memorial Trust, 2004.

Makdisi, George. *Religion, Law and Learning in Classical Islam*. London: Variorum, 1991.

———. *The Rise of Colleges: Institutions of Learning in Islam and the West*. Edinburgh: Edinburgh University Press, 1981.

Young, M. J. L. et al., ed. *Religion, Learning and Science in the 'Abbasid Period*. Cambridge: Cambridge University Press, 1990.

Literature and Literary History

Ashtiany (Bray), Julia, et al., ed. *'Abbasid Belles-Lettres*. Cambridge: Cambridge University Press, 1990.

Bencheikh, Jamel Eddine *Poétique arabe*, 2nd ed. Paris: Gallimard, 1989.

Cooperson, Michael, and Shawkat M. Toorawa, ed. *Arabic Literary Culture, 500–925*. Detroit: Thomson Gale, 2005.

DeYoung, Terri, and Mary St Germain, ed. *Essays in Arabic Literary Biography, 925–1350*. Wiesbaden: Harrassowitz, 2011.

Myrne, Pernilla. *Narrative, Gender and Authority in 'Abbāsid Literature on Women*. Göteborg: University of Gothenburg, 2010.

Music and Song

Bencheikh, Jamel Eddine. "Les musiciens et la poésie. Les écoles d'Isḥāq al-Mawṣilī et d'Ibrāhīm Ibn al-Mahdī." *Arabica*, 22 (1975): 114–52.

Gordon, Matthew S. "The Place of Competition: The Careers of 'Arīb al-Ma'mūniya and 'Ulayya bint al-Mahdī, Sisters in Song." In *'Abbasid Studies: Occasional Papers of the School of Abbasid Studies, Cambridge, 6–10 July 2002*, edited by James E. Montgomery. Leuven: Peeters, 2004.

Samarai, Nicola Lauré al-. *Die Macht der Darstellung. Gender, sozialer Status, historiographischer Re-Präsentation: zwei Frauenbiographien in der frühen Abbasidenzeit.* Wiesbaden: Dr. Ludwig Reichert Verlag, 2001.

Sawa, George. *Music Performance Practice in the Early Abbasid Era 132–320 AH/750–932 AD*, 2nd ed. Toronto: Institute of Medieval Music, 2004.

The Saljūqs

Ḥusaynī, Ṣadr al-Dīn ibn Nāṣir. *Akhbār al-dawlah al-Saljūqiyyah. The History of the Seljuq State.* Translation and commentary by C. E. Bosworth. London: Routledge, 2011.

Lange, Christian, and Söngul Mecit, ed. *The Seljuqs: Politics, Society and Culture.* Edinburgh: Edinburgh University Press, 2011.

Morgan, David O., and Anthony Reid, ed. *The New Cambridge History of Islam. Vol. 2: The Eastern Islamic World, Eleventh to Eighteenth Centuries.* Cambridge: Cambridge University Press, 2010.

Peacock, A. C. S. *The Great Seljuk Empire.* Edinburgh: Edinburgh University Press, 2015.

Renterghem, Vanessa van. "Controlling and Developing Baghdad: Caliphs, Sultans and the Balance of Power in the Abbasid Capital (Mid-5th/11th to Late 6th/12th Centuries)." In *The Seljuqs: Politics, Society and Culture*, edited by Christian Lange and Söngul Mecit, 117–38. Edinburgh: Edinburgh University Press, 2011.

Slaves and Slavery

Bray, Julia. "Men, Women and Slaves in Abbasid society." In *Gender in the Early Medieval World: East and West, 300–900*, edited by Leslie Brubaker and Julia M. H. Smith, 121–46. Cambridge: Cambridge University Press, 2004.

Gordon, Matthew S. and Kathryn A. Hain, ed. *Concubines and Courtesans: Women and Slavery in Islamic History*. Oxford: Oxford University Press, 2017.

Kilpatrick, Hilary. "Women as Poets and Chattels. Abū l-Farağ al-Iṣbahānī's *Al-imā' al-šawā'ir*." *Quaderni di Studi Arabi*, 9 (1991): 161–76.

Popovic, Alexandre. *La révolte des esclaves en Iraq au IIIe/IX siècle*. Paris: P. Geuthner, 1976.

Women

Abbott, Nabia. *Two Queens of Baghdad: Mother and Wife of Hārūn al-Rashīd*. Chicago: University of Chicago Press, 1946.

El Cheikh, Nadia. "Caliphal Harems, Household Harems: Baghdad in the Fourth Century of the Islamic Era." In *Harem Histories: Envisioning Places and Living Spaces*, edited by Marilyn Booth, 87–103. Durham: Duke University Press, 2010.

Hanne, Eric J. "Women, Power, and the Eleventh and Twelfth Century Abbasid Court." *Hawwa: Journal of Women of the Middle East and the Islamic World*, 3 (2005): 80–110.

Roded, Ruth. *Women in Islamic Biographical Collections: From Ibn Sa'd to Who's Who*. Boulder, CO: L. Rienner Publishers, 1994.

Index

About the NYU Abu Dhabi Institute

The Library of Arabic Literature is supported by a grant from the NYU Abu Dhabi Institute, a major hub of intellectual and creative activity and advanced research. The Institute hosts academic conferences, workshops, lectures, film series, performances, and other public programs directed both to audiences within the UAE and to the worldwide academic and research community. It is a center of the scholarly community for Abu Dhabi, bringing together faculty and researchers from institutions of higher learning throughout the region.

NYU Abu Dhabi, through the NYU Abu Dhabi Institute, is a world-class center of cutting-edge research, scholarship, and cultural activity. The Institute creates singular opportunities for leading researchers from across the arts, humanities, social sciences, sciences, engineering, and the professions to carry out creative scholarship and conduct research on issues of major disciplinary, multidisciplinary, and global significance.

About the Translators

Shawkat M. Toorawa is Professor of Arabic in the Department of Near Eastern Languages & Civilizations at Yale University, where he teaches classical Arabic, Arabic literature, the Arabic humanities, and literatures of the world. His current interests include: Qur'anic hapaxes and rhyme-words; the literary and writerly culture of Abbasid Baghdad; the Waqwaq Tree and islands; the 18th-century Indian author Āzād Bilgrāmī; modern poetry; Creole-language Mauritian literature; and SF film and literature. His books include *Ibn Abī Ṭāhir Ṭayfūr: A Ninth-Century Bookman in Baghdad* (2004, paper 2010); a revision/translation of Gregor Schoeler's *The Aural and the Read: The Genesis of Literature in Islam* (2009); and the forthcoming *The Qur'an: Literary Dimensions.*

Julia Bray is the Laudian Professor of Arabic in the University of Oxford, and a fellow of St. John's College. She writes on medieval to early modern Arabic literature, life-writing, and social history, has contributed to the *New Cambridge History of Islam* (2010), to *Essays in Arabic Literary Biography 1350–1850* (2009) and to cross-cultural studies such as *Approaches to the Byzantine Family* (2013), and has edited *Writing and Representation in Medieval Islam* (2006).

Michael Cooperson is Professor of Arabic language and literature at UCLA. He has translated Abdelfattah Kilito's *The Author and His Doubles*, Khairy Shalaby's *Time Travels of the Man Who Sold Pickles and Sweets*, and Jurji Zaidan's *The Caliph's Heirs: Brothers at War*. He is a co-author, with the RRAALL group, of *Interpreting the Self: Autobiography in the Arabic Literary Tradition*; and co-editor, with Shawkat Toorawa, of *The Dictionary of Literary Biography*'s *Arabic Literary Culture, 500–925*. Most recently, he edited and translated *Virtues of the Imām Aḥmad ibn Ḥanbal, Volume One* (2013) and *Volume Two* (2015) for the Library of Arabic Literature.

Philip F. Kennedy is Professor of Middle Eastern and Islamic Studies and Comparative Literature at New York University and Vice Provost for Public Programming for the NYU Abu Dhabi Institute. As author or editor, Kennedy has published several writings on Arabic literature, including *Scheherazade's Children* (2013), co-edited with Marina Warner , and most recently *Recognition in the Arabic Narrative Tradition* (2016).

Joseph E. Lowry is Associate Professor of Arabic and Islamic studies in the Department of Near Eastern Languages and Civilizations at the University of Pennsylvania. His publications include *Early Islamic Legal Theory* (2007) on the scholarship of jurist al-Shāfiʿī and an edition and translation of al-Shāfiʿī's *Epistle on Legal Theory* (2013) for the Library of Arabic Literature.

James E. Montgomery is Sir Thomas Adams's Professor of Arabic at the University of Cambridge and Fellow of Trinity Hall. He is the author of numerous works on Arabic letters, including most recently *Two Arabic Travel Books: Ibn Faḍlān, Mission to the Volga* (2014), for the Library of Arabic Literature, and recently *Al-Jāḥiẓ: In Praise of Books* (2013), and Ibn Faḍlān's *Mission to the Volga* (2014) for the Library of Arabic Literature

Tahera Qutbuddin is Associate Professor of Arabic Literature at the University of Chicago. Her scholarship focuses on intersections of the literary, the religious, and the political in classical Arabic poetry and prose. She was awarded a fellowship from the Carnegie Corporation of New York for her current research on Arabic oratory (*khaṭābah*). She is the author of *Al-Mu'ayyad al-Shīrāzī and Fatimid Daʿwa Poetry: A Case of Commitment in Classical Arabic Literature* (2005) and editor and translator of *A Treasury of Virtues: Sayings, Sermons, and Teachings of ʿAlī* (2013) for the Library of Arabic Literature.

Chip Rossetti is the Editorial Director of the Library of Arabic Literature. He has a Ph.D. in Arabic literature from the University of Pennsylvania. He has translated a number of Arabic novels, including Sonallah Ibrahim's *Beirut, Beirut* (2014), Ahmed Khaled Towfik's *Utopia* (2013), and Magdy El Shafee's graphic novel *Metro* (2012). In 2010, he won a PEN America Translation Fund grant for his translation of Muhammad Makhzangi's short story collection *Animals in Our Days.*

Devin J. Stewart is Associate Professor of Arabic and Islamic Studies at Emory University. His research interests include Islamic law, the Qur'an, Islamic sectarian relations, medieval Arabic prose literature, Islamic biography and autobiography, and Arabic dialects. He has written on the Qur'an, Shi'i Islam, and Islamic legal education, and is most recently the editor-translator of *Disagreements of the Jurists: A Manual of Islamic Legal Theory* (2015) for the Library of Arabic Literature.

The Library of Arabic Literature

For more details on individual titles, visit www.libraryofarabicliterature.org.

Classical Arabic Literature: A Library of Arabic Literature Anthology
Selected and translated by Geert Jan van Gelder

A Treasury of Virtues: Sayings, Sermons and Teachings of ʿAlī, by al-Qāḍī al-Quḍāʿī with the *One Hundred Proverbs* attributed to al-Jāḥiẓ
Edited and translated by Tahera Qutbuddin

The Epistle on Legal Theory, by al-Shāfiʿī
Edited and translated by Joseph E. Lowry

Leg over Leg, by Aḥmad Fāris al-Shidyāq
Edited and translated by Humphrey Davies

Virtues of the Imām Aḥmad ibn Ḥanbal, by Ibn al-Jawzī
Edited and translated by Michael Cooperson

The Epistle of Forgiveness, by Abū l-ʿAlāʾ al-Maʿarrī
Edited and translated by Geert Jan van Gelder and Gregor Schoeler

The Principles of Sufism, by ʿĀʾishah al-Bāʿūniyyah
Edited and translated by Th. Emil Homerin

The Expeditions: An Early Biography of Muḥammad, by Maʿmar ibn Rāshid
Edited and translated by Sean W. Anthony

Two Arabic Travel Books
Accounts of China and India, by Abū Zayd al-Sīrāfī
Edited and translated by Tim Mackintosh-Smith

Mission to the Volga, by Aḥmad ibn Faḍlān
Edited and translated by James Montgomery

Disagreements of the Jurists: A Manual of Islamic Legal Theory, by al-Qāḍī al-Nuʿmān
Edited and translated by Devin J. Stewart

Consorts of the Caliphs: Women and the Court of Baghdad, by Ibn al-Sāʿī
Edited by Shawkat M. Toorawa and translated by the Editors of the Library of Arabic Literature

What ʿĪsā ibn Hishām Told Us, by Muḥammad al-Muwayliḥī
Edited and translated by Roger Allen

The Life and Times of Abū Tammām, by Abū Bakr Muḥammad ibn Yaḥyā al-Ṣūlī
Edited and translated by Beatrice Gruendler

The Sword of Ambition: Bureaucratic Rivalry in Medieval Egypt, by ʿUthmān ibn Ibrāhīm al-Nābulusī
Edited and translated by Luke Yarbrough

Brains Confounded by the Ode of Abū Shādūf Expounded, by Yūsuf al-Shirbīnī
Edited and translated by Humphrey Davies

Light in the Heavens: Sayings of the Prophet Muḥammad, by al-Qāḍī al-Quḍāʿī
Edited and translated by Tahera Qutbuddin

Risible Rhymes, by Muḥammad ibn Maḥfūẓ al-Sanhūrī
Edited and translated by Humphrey Davies

A Hundred and One Nights
Edited and translated by Bruce Fudge

The Excellence of the Arabs, by Ibn Qutaybah
Edited by James E. Montgomery and Peter Webb
Translated by Sarah Bowen Savant and Peter Webb

Scents and Flavors: A Syrian Cookbook
Edited and translated by Charles Perry

Arabian Satire: Poetry from 18th-Century Najd, by Ḥmēdān al-Shwēʿir
Edited and translated by Marcel Kurpershoek

English-only Paperbacks

Leg over Leg: Volumes One and Two, by Aḥmad Fāris al-Shidyāq

Leg over Leg: Volumes Three and Four, by Aḥmad Fāris al-Shidyāq

The Expeditions: An Early Biography of Muḥammad, by Maʿmar ibn Rāshid

The Epistle on Legal Theory: A Translation of al-Shāfiʿī's Risālah, by al-Shāfiʿī

The Epistle of Forgiveness, by Abū l-ʿAlāʾ al-Maʿarrī

The Principles of Sufism, by ʿĀʾishah al-Bāʿūniyyah

A Treasury of Virtues: Sayings, Sermons and Teachings of ʿAlī, by al-Qāḍī al-Quḍāʿī with *The One Hundred Proverbs*, attributed to al-Jāḥiẓ

The Life of Ibn Ḥanbal, by Ibn al-Jawzī

Mission to the Volga, by Ibn Faḍlān

Accounts of China and India, by Abū Zayd al-Sīrāfī

Consorts of the Caliphs: Women and the Court of Baghdad, by Ibn al-Sāʿī

A Hundred and One Nights

Disagreements of the Jurists: A Manual of Islamic Legal Theory, by al-Qāḍī al-Nuʿmān

Lightning Source UK Ltd.
Milton Keynes UK
UKHW010559120419
340921UK00001B/176/P

9 781479 866793